Soup Ki...

Soup Kitchen

Introduction by Hugh Fearnley-Whittingstall

The ultimate collection from the ultimate chefs including Nigella Lawson, Jamie Oliver, Gordon Ramsay and Rick Stein

Edited by **Annabel Buckingham** and **Thomasina Miers**

Dedicated to our long-suffering parents – Mike & Jules and
Probyn & Niki. You are simply wonderful – thank you for your
endless support.

And of course to Noel Hennessy, without whom none of
this would have happened.

First published in 2005 by Collins
an imprint of HarperCollins Publishers
77–85 Fulham Palace Road
London w6 8jb

This paperback edition published 2007

www.collins.co.uk

Collins is a registered trademark of HarperCollins Publishers Ltd

11	10	09	08	07
5	4	3	2	1

Text © various contributors 2005
Introduction © Hugh Fearnley-Whittingstall 2005
Photography © Richard Learoyd 2005

Design: George Lewis
Photographer: Richard Learoyd
Editor: Susan Fleming

A catalogue record for this book is available from the British Library

ISBN-13 978-0-00-725538-2

Colour reproduction by Colourscan, Singapore
Printed and bound by Printing Express Ltd, Hong Kong

www.soupkitchen.org

Contents

Foreword

This book is the result of a year's work and an incredible journey. We were somewhat cautious about taking it on (we had known each other only two months and had no experience of the publishing world and no funding for the project) but there was an inevitability about the book right from the start and we both felt a tremendous excitement about making it happen. Undeterred by the obstacles (Annabel couldn't cook and Tommi knew nothing about design) we speed-read the *Writers and Artists' Yearbook* in an afternoon and got on the phone to talk to chefs about soup. The results amazed even optimists like us. Within a week we had 12 recipes, by the next we had 40.

Friends have rallied round to make encouraging noises and share invaluable pearls of wisdom. They have advised us on everything from book clubs to corporate sponsorship and copyright law and have never laughed at our staggering ignorance (as we toasted our first publishing offer, we suddenly realised that we weren't totally sure what a royalty was). Our parents have lovingly refrained from telling us to get normal jobs. Outstanding professionals including a photographer, graphic designer, law firm, literary agent, accountancy firm and website design company have offered to work with us and represent us for free (please see page 224 for our full list of contributing stars).

It's been a trip. We've found ourselves in some amazing situations – from slick publishing houses and star-studded launches to incredible soup kitchens and blooming allotments. We've donned suits at Book Fairs, worn blue hairnets and white coats at the Maldon salt vats and spent many hours brainstorming over a latte at Carluccios. We hope this book conveys something of the amazing story which has included bumping into Jamie Oliver filming at La Fromagerie and meeting Oliver Peyton as he popped in for a sandwich at EAT. Oh, and Tommi entered and won MasterChef.

The motivation behind this collection is to raise money for the varied and wonderful work of homeless charities across the UK through the talents of a fantastic collection of chefs. Over half the chefs have taken the time to create an original recipe for us. We hope this book will make you want to cook and, we hope, you will love using it as much as we've loved creating it.

Annabel and Tommi
www.soupkitchen.org.uk

P.S. There is no such thing as the definitive collection. For the chefs we haven't asked, we can only apologize. We're already blushing at the gaps.

Introduction
by Hugh Fearnley-Whittingstall

What is soup? Clearly it takes many forms. From a snack or a starter to a full blown supper, from a delicate but intense transparent infusion, to something so thick and robust you might want to swap your spoon for a knife and fork. Really, there is no more versatile dish on the planet. This explains soup's unique ability to cut across all the cultural boundaries of food, and delight the palates of men, women and children wherever they gather to share food.

Soup not only thrills the taste buds of diners the world over, it also stretches the imagination, and mediates the feelings, of all who love to cook. Sometimes it's a blend of subtle and extravagant ingredients fine tuned by a maverick genius to whet the appetite of a millionaire – for another seven courses to come. And sometimes it's a gloriously homey mix of vegetables, meat and seasoning served up by a devoted mother to a bickering family who may pause, almost imperceptibly and without self-awareness, to taste her love before resuming the fight. In both cases – in almost all cases – soup is demonstrative, honest, guileless, and dearly appreciated.

More prosaically, but importantly, soups are generally very healthy too. So often based on an encouraging, upbeat mix of fresh vegetables (with the protein element more of a spice than a staple) they are invariably enjoyed by those who may be sceptical of the same ingredients presented in a less heart-warming manner. They are therefore a brilliant way to ensure the bodies of our loved ones are getting the vitamins and minerals they need.

Soups naturally lend themselves to the undeniable virtues of sourcing locally, and cooking seasonally. In fact, one of your best options for creating a quick and rewarding meal is to reach for three or four fresh seasonal vegetables, wash and prepare them as appropriate, and simmer them in some well-seasoned stock. Such a naturally improvised soup is rarely anything less than a pleasure. And with the addition of a little chopped leftover meat, some lentils or beans perhaps, pasta or rice, some toasted or fried bread croûtons, maybe a bit of grated cheese (really any, some, or all of these things), you are well into the realms of deep comfort and total satisfaction.

And soups are mostly excellent value for money. Leftovers are rich pickings, so that food that might otherwise go to waste can be reincarnated–often in a form that transcends the original. This means you can be magnanimous to your family and friends, even with

meagre resources. They are also surprisingly portable, being able to travel almost anywhere you might consider taking a mug or flask of tea or coffee. You can eat soup at your desk at work, in front of the telly, on a bus or a boat, on a picnic (especially under a brolly in the rain).

As you will doubtless find as you explore the recipes in this book, soups are easy to make. This collection has been put together with contributions from the most talented and inspired chefs and cooks working in Britain today. Most of them are, if they put their minds to it, quite capable of baffling you with obscure ingredients and frustrating you with demanding techniques. But they won't do so here. Soup confounds attempts to be arcane or vainglorious in the kitchen. It finds even top flight cooks at their most relaxed and informal. The recipes in this collection are for the finest soups of the finest chefs. But they are easy going, down to earth and very, very do-able.

I know this, as it happens, because I've already been doing a few of them myself. I have particularly enjoyed Henry Harris's effortlessly hearty Cannellini Bean and Smoked Haddock (page 203), and the delightfully tangy and irresistibly purple Soup of Five Tomatoes and Three Beetroots by Sally Clarke (page 160). It's been a pleasure to read Shaun Hill's no nonsense approach to the often divisive subject of fish soup (page 182). And Aaron Patterson's outstanding mushroom soup (page 38) has swept away a long-held aversion to the genre caused by youthful encounters with tins. I can see many treats ahead too. For example, I'm looking forward to comparing and contrasting the innovative presence of sausage in Nigella Lawson's Yellow Split Pea and Frankfurter soup, and Sam and Sam Clarke's Chestnut and Chorizo.

So please, like me, make this a working cookbook in a busy kitchen. Get it a bit soupy. Approach the recipes without fear. In fact, you could do a lot worse than bear in mind the well-chosen words of Fergus Henderson, from the introduction to his lovely book, *Nose to Tail Eating*:

"Do not be afraid of cooking as your ingredients will know, and misbehave. Enjoy your cooking and the food will behave; moreover it will pass your pleasure on to those who eat it."

Perhaps a good way of summarising the numerous and considerable virtues of soup is to say that it is always among the most generous and friendly of dishes. And that is why it has been chosen as the subject of a book with the most generous and friendly of intentions. The editors, Annabel and Thomasina, have put this collection together with the aim of raising much-needed funds for the homeless. Their amazing energy and enthusiasm, and inexhaustible optimism for the project, have been inspiring. In wholehearted support of this venture, every chef has given their time and contribution for free. This spirit of giving, above all things, forms the essence of the collection.

So we hope you too will be generous with this book, as with your soup-making. Buy a few extra copies, and dish them out. They're sure to slip down a treat.

Soup Stocks

Stocks

Stocks are a clever dichotomy in the art of cooking. On the one hand making a stock is saving and making use of every scrap left over from a roast, every last drop of flavour from a decimated carcass. As Hugh would say, it is meat thrift: why chuck out bones and bits that could be a building ingredient to a whole other meal? Making stocks also partly justifies the animal's slaughter in the first place, as one is not complacently throwing away the tasty morsels and bones that could otherwise feed a family all over again. On the other hand, stock can be a wildly extravagant thing; making the stock is the start to building up a dish – the dish being the excuse for the stock rather than the other way round. You would be hard pressed to find a Michelin-starred kitchen without at least two different stocks bubbling away every day, sometimes many more to make up their rich, truffled sauces.

Though stocks are integral to many stews, terrines, risottos and sauces, they will always lend most obviously to making that wholesome and simple meal-in-one, the soup. A good stock renders an otherwise insipid bowl of meat, vegetables, pasta or grain into a thing fit for a king. It is even good with some bean dishes (it is a well-guarded secret that home-made baked beans have the same powers as Cupid, when made with a top-notch stock, of course. If you don't believe it, try the recipe on our website). And, best of all, stock is an absolute doddle to make. Whether using leftover carcasses or specifically making a stock from fresh bones, the largest ingredient required following the bones of the particular animal is water followed by some choice vegetables and herbs. In the case of using fresh bones, rather than those left over from some feast, most quality butchers and fishmongers are normally only too happy to give bones away for a song. With an eye to few basic principles, you should find that your stock will rarely disappoint. These include:

Be generous with the vegetables and herbs – in quantity and quality
Use fresh vegetables that you would want to eat for supper. These will make your soup supreme. Carrots and onions are always essential building-blocks to a soup because of their high sugar levels and rich flavours. After that you can play around a bit with herbs (parsley is always good, ditto bay leaves, and thyme is delicious) and other vegetables such as celery, green vegetables and even the roots, though be careful of using too much celeriac or turnip which can overpower a stock. A few whole peppercorns add a nice piquancy too.

Pack 'em tight
Cut up your vegetables to allow the most flavour out, and ram them into the stockpot. Get a meat cleaver and cut up the bones. Squeeze all the bits in a saucepan that will just about fit the goodies comfortably and cover with water. If you drown your stock items in

water, the flavour will be reflected in a less concentrated taste. Top up with boiling water as you need to so that everything is always covered, releasing delicious flavours.

Simmer constantly

Put your stock on to heat until it reaches a lovely, gentle simmer, or as Hugh would put it, a 'tremulous simmer'. If you maintain it at this level, your stock will take on all the flavours of your ingredients without becoming cloudy and discoloured. For a fresh, top-notch stock, simmer for 4-5 hours. If you are using tired bones and veg, then 2 hours will do. In either case, never simmer for much longer than 5 hours, or you will destroy the fine flavour of your brew.

Taste and adjust

Once you've made your stock, strain out the base ingredients. It is worth straining the stock again through a fine sieve or chinois, to get rid of all the small particles. This is important when you are adjusting the strength of your stock. If the flavour is too weak, you will need to boil it a bit to reduce its volume and strengthen its flavour. If particles remain in the soup, boiling them will result in a bitter, insipid flavour to the broth. The more you reduce, the more the flavour intensifies. If you wish to freeze your stock for later use, reduce the stock until it's dark and gelatinous and freeze in ice-cube trays to make the perfect home-made stock cube, a million miles from ones bought in the supermarket.

NB Never add salt to a stock, as you never know what strength (and therefore volume) you are aiming for until the end; reducing a seasoned stock will intensify the salty taste. Only season once the stock has been added to your soup.

A good home-made stock

You can tell a good stock, as it will gel in its bowl once it has chilled. The sight of that jelliness is the rewards of the work you have put into your stock. That jelliness is something to be proud of. Forget strawberry-flavoured jellies when you were small – nothing beats the feeling of creating this one. There in your fridge or freezer sits the most vital of ingredients for your home-made soup (and it will teach you how to win friends and influence people).

Bought stocks

If you really can't face making your own stock, nowadays you can buy some pretty upmarket replacements which, whilst not delivering the full punch of your home-made variety, will make up for it to a certain extent. You will, of course, have to pay for this privilege. As for stock cubes, these are cheaper, and let's face it, easy to chuck into a soup for some added flavour. Some bouillon cubes are of a higher quality than supermarket own brand labels, but be warned, if you use these cubes over a period of time, you too will start to detect a level of 'sameness' pervading even your most luxurious soups.

Vegetable Stock

There are many versions of vegetable stock, but this one is quite gutsy.

Makes about 1.5 litres

2 large onions, studded with a few cloves, cut in chunks
4 carrots, cut in chunks
3 celery stalks, cut into chunks
1 fennel bulb, sliced
4 cabbage leaves, chopped
2 leeks, washed and roughly chopped
1 bouquet garni (see below)
zest of 1 lemon
5 black peppercorns
2 litres water

Put all the ingredients in a stockpot and bring to a simmer. Simmer for a couple of hours, topping up with water as needed, so the ingredients are always covered.

Strain, cool and use! Or freeze.

Note

A bouquet garni is a bunch of herbs used to flavour soups and sauces. A bouquet normally consists of parsley, thyme and a few dried bay leaves, but can be adapted as creatively as you wish. Normally tied together in a bundle so that the herbs don't escape, and so that they can be deftly removed just before serving (unless you buy the little, ready-prepared sachets from grocers or supermarkets). NB If you are making your own bouquet, never be tempted to use an elastic band to tie it together – it will leave a horrible, plastic flavour to your broth. String is much more advisable (but not blue).

Beef Stock

Beef shin is particularly good in a beef stock, as are the ribs and leg. Bones are what give the rich, gelatinous feel we're searching for.

Makes about 1.5-2 litres depending on size of pot and timing

2.5kg beef bones
2 onions, unpeeled and quartered
2 carrots, chopped
2 leeks, washed and chopped
1 tbsp vegetable oil
1 bouquet garni (see page 19)
10 black peppercorns

Preheat the oven to 200ºC/Gas 6. Wash the bones thoroughly and roast for half an hour with the onion until well browned.

Sauté the veggies in oil in the stockpot until taking up a bit of colour, and then add the bones and onion. Cover with water and add the bouquet garni and peppercorns. Cover with water and bring to the boil. Simmer gently for 3-5 hours, skimming off scum as it emerges, and topping up with hot water.

Strain well, the second time through a fine chinois, and cool. Refrigerate and skim off the fat. If you wish to freeze the stock, put back in a clean saucepan and simmer to reduce quantity, intensifying the flavour. Pour into a few ice-cube trays and freeze your home-made stock cubes.

Chicken Stock

Probably the most useful of all kinds of stock, a chicken stock will add flavour to anything from a sauce to a risotto or stew and, of course, many soup recipes, provided you are not cooking for vegetarians. If it is really well made you can drink it neat too. The most obvious way to make a chicken stock is by using the bones and leftovers from a roast, but if you are making a stock from a fresh, raw chicken, just throw the chicken in a 180ºC/Gas 4 oven for 15 minutes to brown it a little and get a bit of flavour in your stock. If you are using a leftover carcass, adding a raw neck of chicken, or gizzard, and some giblets will add to the flavour and depth. If you want a stronger stock, simmer to reduce. You will have less liquid than designated below, but it will have a richer flavour.

Makes 1-1.5 litres, depending on size of pot and bird

**1 cooked chicken carcass, with all the leftover
gunk (skin, fat, jelly, ooze)
1 large onion, or 2 medium, with a few cloves stuck in,
cut in chunks
2 carrots, cut in chunks
2 celery stalks, cut in chunks
3 black peppercorns
1 bouquet garni (see page 19)
2 garlic cloves (optional)**

Put all the ingredients in a large pot (big enough to fit ingredients, but with not much spare room), and cover with water. Bring to a gentle simmer and simmer for up to 5 hours, but no longer, or leave in a very low warm oven overnight (100ºC). Skim away any grey scum as it comes to the surface (which contain impurities), and keep topping up with hot water as the water evaporates so that the goods are always covered.

Strain and cool, skimming off any fat that rises to the surface. Chill or freeze.

Game Stock

Follow the chicken stock recipe but using a game bird instead of a chicken. Add 3 juniper berries to the stock and simmer as directed. Good for making terrines and game stews.

Fish Stock

Fish stock is wonderful as it can't be cooked for longer than 20 minutes, or the fish bones impart a horrid, bitter flavour to the stock. Fish stock is therefore a brilliantly quick thing to make, and once mastered can be done simultaneously to any main dish with no trouble at all, to add depth of flavour to fish stews, soups, sauces etc. It's very good fast food.

Makes 1 litre

700g white fish bones (heads, bits, bones etc)
½ fennel bulb, chopped
1 onion, chopped
1 carrot, chopped
1 leek, washed and chopped
2 tbsp olive oil
zest of 1 lemon
1 bouquet garni (see page 19)
250ml white wine

Rinse the fish bones well under a running tap. Cook the veggies in olive oil without colouring (i.e. sweat) for about 10 minutes. Add the bones and all the remaining ingredients, and boil to reduce in volume by a third. Cover with water and bring up to a simmer, skimming any scum that rises, and cook at a simmer for 20 minutes. Any longer and the fish bones will emit a bitter, unpleasant flavour to your stock. You want a beautifully light flavoured liquid.

Sieve (you will need to use a chinois to get rid of finer particles) and use, but don't keep in the fridge for longer than a day.

Autumn

Sweetcorn, Damsons and Plums, Blackberries, Mutton, Apples, Partridge, Wood Pigeon, Venison, Oysters, Cucumber, Spinach, Figs, Grouse, Mussels, Sea Bass, Onion, Elderberries, Watercress, Beetroot, Mushrooms, Marrow, Kale, Pumpkin, Squash, Sweet Potato, Goose, Jerusalem Artichokes, Chicory, Clementines, English White Celery, Turbot, Chestnuts, Cranberries, Swede, Potatoes, Teal, Parsnips, Pears, Leeks, Quinces, Turkey, Pomegranate, Red Cabbage, Wild Duck, Celeriac, Turnips, Sprouts, Porcini Mushrooms

Michel Roux

Le Gavroche, Mayfair, London

Squash and Shrimp Soup with Nutmeg

If using small squash, the soup can be served in the hollowed-out skins, or a big pumpkin can be brought to the table as a tureen.

Serves 4

4 x 175g squash or 1 x 700g pumpkin, unpeeled weight
4 shallots
2 tbsp olive oil
salt and pepper to taste
freshly grated nutmeg
1 litre good Chicken or Vegetable Stock (see page 21 or 19)
200g peeled brown shrimps

If using the squash or pumpkin for serving this soup, slice off the top and hollow out the flesh and seeds using a spoon. Otherwise, cut away the skin with a knife. Cut the flesh into very small dice. Peel and chop the shallots.

Sweat the vegetables in a little olive oil until soft but not coloured. Season with a generous amount of salt, pepper and nutmeg, then pour in the chicken stock. Bring to a simmer and cook for 20 minutes, then blend until smooth.

Add the shrimps just before serving.

Bruce Poole
Chez Bruce

Roast chicken, wild mushroom and onion soup

Probably serves about 4 really greedy bastards (or 8 nancies) as a starter.

Joint a chicken, divide the legs and drummers into two, and chop up the carcass. In a big cast-iron pan, brown the pieces in butter (but not the breasts) together with the carcass (and ideally a pig's trotter if you happen to have one - if you are Jewish, you may not). Season the chicken really well. When the chicken is really dark golden, remove and reserve.

In the same pan reserve a little fat and sweat 3 finely sliced (not chopped) onions with 2-3 garlic cloves until well caramelised – this will take at least half an hour. Keep scraping the pan as you go to prevent catching, and then season the onions. When softened and caramelised, add half a bottle of white wine or dry cider and boil down until nearly all the liquid has evaporated.

Add back the chicken pieces and carcass and cover with ideally chicken stock (or water).Throw in a couple of bay leaves and a big bunch of thyme. When the soup comes to a very gentle simmer, skim well twice.

Cook very gently for about an hour, then fish out the chicken pieces and carcass; throw out the carcass and the trotter, if used. Discard the herbs too.

Sauté the chicken breasts really well, skin-side down, so they go a nice dark golden colour. Deglaze your sauté pan with a splash of soup and return both (i.e. breasts and the residue from the sauté pan) back to the soup. Skim the soup again.

Sauté a generous pan of wild mushrooms (whatever is around, buttons are also good, but you will need plenty), season well and drain after cooking. Throw the mushrooms (the more the merrier) into the soup.

Serve when the chicken breasts are cooked: they take very little time - about 10 minutes at a very gentle simmer. (On no account boil them or they will end up dry.) Take out the breasts and carve each into 3 pieces.

Delicious. Adjust the seasoning, stir in a handful of chopped fresh tarragon and flat parsley, and serve at once with crusty bread. Or with some gnocchi or noodles as a tasty lunch.

Sam Clark and Sam Clark
Moro, Clerkenwell, London

Chestnut and Chorizo Soup/Sopa de Castañas

Forests of sweet chestnut thrive in the mountainous regions of Spain. This recipe combines some of the classic flavours of Spanish cooking to produce a warm, comforting and mildly spicy soup that is synonymous with the onset of autumn.

Serves 4

4 tbsp olive oil
1 large Spanish onion, diced
1 medium carrot, diced
1 celery stalk, thinly sliced
120g mild cooking chorizo, cut into 1cm cubes
salt and pepper to taste
2 garlic cloves, thinly sliced
1 tsp ground cumin
1½ tsp finely chopped fresh thyme leaves

2 small dried red chillies, crushed
2 tomatoes, fresh or tinned, roughly chopped
500g cooked peeled chestnuts
(fresh or vacuum-packed), roughly chopped
20 saffron strands, infused in 3-4 tbsp boiling water
1 litre water

In a large saucepan, heat the oil over a medium heat. Add the onion, carrot, celery, chorizo and a pinch of salt and fry for about 20 minutes, stirring occasionally, until everything caramelises and turns quite brown. This gives the soup a wonderfully rich colour and taste.

Now add the garlic, cumin, thyme and chilli and cook for 1 more minute, followed by the tomato and, after about 2 minutes, the chestnuts. Give everything a good stir, then add the saffron-infused liquid and the water, and simmer for about 10 minutes.

Remove from the heat and mash by hand (with a potato masher) until almost smooth but still with a little bit of texture. Season with salt and pepper.

(From *Moro The Cookbook*, Ebury Press, 2001)

Hugh Fearnley-Whittingstall
Food writer, River Cottage

Roast Pumpkin Soup with Crispy Garlic

I've always liked pumpkins and squashes made into a soup, and I love them roasted too. This year, thinking how delicious the flavours are that you get when you roast peppers and tomatoes, and what good soup that makes, I decided on a similar approach with my favourite squash varieties. The result was gorgeous. You can use any pumpkin or squash for this soup, and the ever-popular butternut works particularly well. But if you can get some of the other sweet squash varieties, such as sweet mama, acorn, or kabocha, generally available from mid-October to late November, then so much the better.

Serves 4

1 medium pumpkin or 2 small squashes
2 tbsp extra virgin olive oil, plus extra for garnish
6 garlic cloves, lightly crushed, plus a few extra
for garnish
salt and pepper to taste
1 litre Chicken or Vegetable Stock (see pages 21
and 19)

Preheat the oven to 200ºC/Gas 6.

There's no need to peel the pumpkin or squashes. Just cut them into rough chunks or thick slices and scrape away the seeds and surrounding soft fibres. Lay the slices in a large roasting tin, and drizzle generously with olive oil. Scatter the garlic cloves, whole with the skin on, over the tray, and season well with salt and pepper.

Put in the preheated oven for 35-40 minutes, turning once or twice if you like, so the pumpkin pieces are well roasted and nicely browned. Use a spoon to scrape the soft flesh of the roasted pumpkin pieces away from the skin. Heat the stock in a pan. Put some of the scraped flesh into a liquidiser, along with the flesh squeezed out from the roasted garlic cloves, and pour in enough hot stock to cover. Liquidise in batches, until completely smooth, returning the soup to a clean pan. Taste the soup

and adjust the seasoning. Add enough stock to get a thick and creamy consistency.

Heat the soup through without re-boiling it, and as you are doing so, fry a few thin slivers of garlic in a little oil. Scatter these thin shards of crisp fried garlic over each bowl of hot soup as you serve it. Finish, if you like, with a trickle of olive oil.

Maxine Clark
Food writer

Jerusalem Artichoke and Parmesan Soup

An unusual combination of mild Jerusalem artichokes with a hint of spice and the nutty taste of Parmesan cheese. The flavour of fresh Parmesan makes this soup really special. Don't be tempted to use the dry cheese sold in cartons, it bears no comparison to the real thing. Spanish pimentón has a strong sweet smoky flavour, but use really good fresh sweet paprika if it is difficult to find. (And throw out your paprika if you have had it more than a year as it will have lost its wonderful fresh aroma.)

Serves 6

450g Jerusalem artichokes
2 shallots
50g butter
1 tsp mild curry paste
900ml Chicken or Vegetable Stock (see pages 21 and 19)
150ml single cream (or milk, but it won't be as rich)
freshly grated nutmeg, to taste
a pinch of smoked paprika (Spanish pimentón)
4 tbsp freshly grated Parmesan
salt and pepper to taste

Melba toast
3-4 slices day-old soft-grain white bread
a little extra freshly grated Parmesan
¼ tsp smoked paprika (Spanish pimentón)

Scrub the Jerusalem artichokes thoroughly to remove any dirt and loose skin. Pat dry then slice thinly. Peel and dice the shallots.

Melt the butter in a large saucepan and add the shallots. Cook gently for 5 minutes until soft and golden. Stir in the curry paste and cook for 1 minute. Add the sliced artichokes and stock and stir well. Bring to the boil, cover and simmer for about 15 minutes or until the artichokes are tender.

Meanwhile, make the Melba toast. Preheat the oven to 180ºC/Gas 4. Toast the bread lightly on both sides. Quickly cut off the crusts and split each slice in two. Scrape off any doughy bits, then sprinkle with Parmesan and paprika. Place on a baking sheet and bake in the preheated oven for 10-15 minutes or until evenly golden. Keep warm.

Add the cream, nutmeg, and paprika to the soup. Transfer to a liquidiser (a blender will not make the soup smooth enough) and liquidise until smooth, then pass through a sieve into a clean saucepan. Reheat the soup and stir in the Parmesan. Taste and adjust the seasoning. Serve with the warm Melba toast.

Mohammed Ourad
Momo, Mayfair, London

Harira

Why we like soup: comforting and warming in the winter, soft and fresh in the spring, spicy and cool in the summer and homely and rich in the autumn. Soup is an all-season affair, which is why we love it. The freshness of the ingredients is paramount. Simplicity is the key, a clever combination of few ingredients can make the mouth water like little else. It's an all-consuming experience. Crusty bread, a glass of good wine and a bowl of soup are tasty, nutritional and satisfying. Soup can be sophisticated, it can be homely. The best restaurants serve complex combinations of rare subtlety (consommé with langoustine tails and bay organic broad beans); at home, we like nothing more than a good harira, a spiced North African vegetable broth, which is usually prepared with lamb, but sometimes chicken too. Harira is the national soup, eaten during the 30 days of Ramadan. Every house prepares this soup, impregnating the streets with its scent at sundown. It is often eaten with dates and honey pastries (briouats).

Serves 10

100g chickpeas
100g lentils
½ tsp bicarbonate of soda
1 x 1kg chicken
100g plain flour
3 tbsp olive oil
150g butter
250g onions, diced
2 celeriac heads, peeled and diced

600g fresh tomatoes, chopped
150g tomato paste
salt and pepper to taste
2 good pinches ras-el-hanout (Moroccan mixed spice)
2 good pinches saffron strands
a big handful of fresh coriander
3 eggs

The day before, soak the chickpeas and lentils separately in cold water with the bicarbonate of soda. Then on the day, just rinse thoroughly and keep to one side.

Burn any remaining feathers and feather stubs from the chicken over the gas flame. Cut it in four pieces, and toss in the seasoned flour.

Heat the oil and butter in a casserole and cook the chicken in this, turning, for about 15 minutes. Add the onion and celeriac dice, and fry gently for another 10 minutes.

Add the chickpeas and lentils, the chopped tomatoes and tomato paste. Add salt, pepper and ras-el-hanout to taste. Cover with 2.5 litres water, and bring to the boil. Add the saffron and let it cook gently for an hour.

Remove the chicken from the pot, and when cool enough to handle, remove and discard the bones and skin. Cut the flesh into small pieces. Put the chicken pieces back into the soup with the chopped coriander. Break the eggs into the soup and stir around for a few minutes.

This soup is always served hot. Some people serve it with fresh dates.

Patricia Michelson

La Fromagerie, Marylebone, London

Golden Onion Soup with Cheese Toasts

The glow from a bowl of soup is both restorative and comforting. It is a loving spoonful on stressful days and at family gatherings. In autumn we see beautiful firm onions and as the days draw in what could put a glow in your cheeks more easily than a bowl of steaming hot soup. The stock is essential. Home-made for preference, but I'll turn a blind eye if you want to use an easier method. If you do this, I can suggest a can or two of chicken consommé will add a richness to the taste.

Stock
1kg chicken carcasses and wings
500g lean shin of beef in one piece
1 veal marrow bone
2 medium onions (not Spanish), skins wiped clean
2 large carrots, scraped
2 leeks, washed and trimmed, keeping some of the green on
2 celery stalks
about 8-10 black peppercorns
1 bouquet garni (bay, marjoram, thyme, parsley)
salt to taste

Soup
1.5kg firm onions
150-180g unsalted butter
100ml white wine (something fruity, not too dry)

Cheese toasts
a few slices day-old bread such as pain de Poilane, sourdough or (my favourite) Italian pagnotta
60ml white wine
2 tbsp grain mustard
100g Comte d'Estive, Emmenthal or Swiss Gruyère cheese

To make the stock, in a large saucepan place the chicken carcasses, beef shin and marrow bone, and cover completely in water (use filtered if possible). Bring to the boil and skim off the scum when necessary, keeping the stock at a rolling boil (i.e. not too fierce). Add all the vegetables and more water to cover completely and return to the boil. Add the peppercorns, bouquet garni and a good few pinches of sea salt (not too much as you can always season to taste later). Cover the pan with a tight-fitting lid and cook gently for at least 2 hours. Strain into a clean bowl.

For the soup, peel the outer skin off the onions and discard. Slice (not chop) the onions thinly. In a large saucepan, melt the butter until foaming and sauté the onions until translucent and golden, but not brown. Over a gentle heat stir the white wine into the buttery golden onions. Ladle in the stock until the

consistency is how you like it (i.e. you may prefer a thicker soup). Gently simmer for 20 minutes

Slice the bread into 'shards' rather than cubes. Dry out in a medium-low oven (150ºC/Gas 2) for about 10 minutes.

Heat the grill to high. Take the pieces of toast and brush with some white wine. Add a smear of grain mustard and top with thick shavings of cheese. Place under the grill on a foil-covered tray until the cheese is bubbling and golden.

Taste the soup for seasoning and ladle into warm soup bowls. Top with the cheese toasts and a sprinkling of chopped flat-leaf parsley (if desired). Wait for that smile to come with each mouthful. Bon appetit à tous.

Aaron Patterson

Hambleton Hall, Oakham, Rutland

Mushroom Soup

Serves 6

100g shiitake mushrooms
100g oyster mushrooms
400g field mushrooms
50g ceps
50g morel mushrooms
3 garlic cloves
5 large shallots
3 fresh thyme sprigs
50g unsalted butter
1 bottle Gewürztraminer (sweet wine)

½ bottle Madeira
600ml Chicken stock (see page 21)
400ml double cream
salt and pepper to taste
juice of 1-2 lemons
50g fresh tarragon, chopped

Prepare the mushrooms by brushing them with a barely damp cloth to get rid of excess dirt. Chop the shiitake, oyster and field, and dice the ceps. Crush the garlic, and finely chop the shallots. Sweat the mushrooms, garlic, shallot and thyme in the butter until softened.

Add the alcohol. Allow to boil for 3 minutes and then add the chicken stock and cream, and boil to reduce by a third. Pass through a fine sieve.

Season with salt, pepper and lemon juice to taste, and add the freshly chopped tarragon at the last moment. Serve.

Graham Grafton
Barnsley House, Barnsley, Gloucestershire

Potato and Cep Soup

This recipe was given to me by Franco Taruschio of Walnut Tree fame, and is a great favourite at Barnsley House. I like it for its sheer simplicity and earthy deliciousness (is that a word?). I hope you enjoy it as much as I do!

Serves 4

5 medium potatoes
salt and pepper to taste
2 garlic cloves
200g fresh ceps
60g butter
250ml double cream
2 tbsp chopped fresh parsley
freshly grated Parmesan

Peel and chop the potatoes. Boil them in salted water with the garlic. Leave the potatoes to cook until they start to disintegrate.

Meanwhile, clean and slice the ceps, and fry them in half the butter.

Pass the potatoes, cooking water and garlic through a food mill. Return to the heat. Add the remaining butter, and some salt and pepper to taste. Beat the mixture with a whisk. If the mixture is too thick, add some water.

A few minutes before serving, add the ceps, cream and parsley to the soup. Serve sprinkled with Parmesan.

Tamasin Day-Lewis
Food writer and Weekend Telegraph food columnist

Spiced Sweet Potato and Red Onion Squash Soup

It is a cliché to say it, but soup is the great comforter. A thick soup on the stove and the smell of a loaf in the oven are as close to paradise as you can get, regardless of the chill or the state of your soul. Both will be assuaged by inner heat after a bowl of this wonderfully and subtly spiced soup. When I first tried it I knew there was something I couldn't identify, deepening and intensifying the flavour. It was the sesame seeds. This is based on a recipe given me by a lovely cook called Nelisha and is from her native Sri Lanka.

Serves 4

30g unsalted butter or 1 tbsp light olive oil
1 medium red onion, finely chopped
2 garlic cloves, finely chopped
1 tsp each of cumin, coriander and sesame seeds, lightly roasted in a pan for 30 seconds
a thumb of fresh root ginger, peeled and chopped
1-2 green chillies, seeded and chopped
finely grated zest and juice of 1 lime
1 tsp honey

1.2 litres Vegetable Stock (see page 19)
360g sweet potato, peeled and diced
360g red onion squash, peeled and diced
a handful of fresh coriander leaves, roughly chopped
salt and pepper to taste

Garnish
150g live yoghurt or 200ml canned coconut milk
olive oil

Heat the butter or oil and cook the onion and garlic gently until softened. Add the spices, ginger, chilli, lime zest and honey, and stir them in. Cook for a minute to amalgamate the flavours.

Add the stock, half the lime juice, the sweet potato, squash and coriander leaves, and bring to the boil. Reduce to a simmer and cook until the vegetables are tender, about 20 minutes.

Liquidise until very smooth, adding more stock to achieve the right consistency. Add the rest of the lime juice, and seasoning if you need to.

Serve with a swirl of yoghurt or coconut milk and a few drops of olive oil.

Jill Dupleix
Cookery editor, The Times

Curried Sweet Potato Soup

This is my favourite sort of soup, one that just tastes sweetly of vegetables and not much else. It doesn't need chicken stock, as it makes its own sweet potato stock as it cooks. The white beans then give it a lush, velvety texture, and the curry powder makes it irresistible. I serve it in a big bowl with a great whacking slice of grilled sourdough bread sticking half in and half out of the bowl. It also dresses up nicely for dinner, with a dollop of soured cream or yoghurt, and some warm Indian naan bread on the side.

Serves 4

1kg orange-fleshed sweet potato
1.2 litres boiling water or stock (see pages 14-23)
salt and pepper to taste
400g canned white beans
1 tsp good curry powder, or more
2 tbsp fresh parsley or coriander leaves

Peel the sweet potatoes and cut into small cubes. Put in a pan, add the boiling water or stock, salt and pepper, and bring to the boil. Simmer for 15 minutes or until the sweet potato is soft.

Drain the beans and rinse. Add half the beans and the curry powder to the soup, stirring well, then whizz in a food processor in batches, being careful not to overfill the bowl.

Return to the pan, add the remaining whole beans, and gently heat. If too thick, add extra boiling water.

Taste for salt, pepper and curry powder, and scatter with parsley or coriander.

Sophie Conran
Food writer

Root Soup with Cheese Scones

I love soup. My kids love soup. They ask me to make it for them at least once a week. It is easy to throw together, and is usually made from whatever I find in the vegetable drawer at the bottom of the fridge, plus any herbs or spices I am in the mood for. A soup is a great way to get a big dose of vegetables: it is soothing, satisfying and worthy of poems.

250g parsnips
250g sweet potatoes
250g carrots
150g red onions
150g leeks
150g celery
1½ tsp cumin seeds
1½ tsp crushed dried chilli
salt and pepper to taste
3 tbsp olive oil

25g butter
1.5 litres water

Cheese scones
150g butter, cut into small cubes
450g plain flour, plus extra for dusting
4 tsp baking powder
300g strong Cheddar, grated
1 tsp mustard powder (optional)
150ml milk

Preheat the oven to 190ºC/Gas 5.

Peel, trim and roughly chop the parsnips, sweet potatoes and carrots. Peel, trim and chop the onions, leeks and celery.

Put half the carrots aside. Put the rest of the carrots, the parsnips and sweet potatoes in a baking tray. Add the spices, salt, pepper and 2 tbsp of the olive oil and shake the tray until all the vegetables are coated with oil. Place in the middle of the oven for up to 45 minutes, checking and turning from time to time until they are brown.

In a large pan add the remaining olive oil and the butter, and put on a gentle heat. Cook the onion until translucent, for about 5 minutes, then add the remaining carrot, with the celery and leeks. Grind over some pepper, cover and soften for 20 minutes, stirring occasionally to make sure it does not burn. If it becomes watery, take off the lid until all the liquid has evaporated.

Add the water, roast vegetables and plenty of salt, and let simmer for a further 10 minutes. Take off the heat and let cool, then liquidise in a food processor.

Meanwhile, for the cheese scones, turn the oven temperature up to 220ºC/ Gas 7.

Add the butter to a large bowl with the flour and baking powder. Rub the butter into the flour between your fingers and thumbs until it looks like breadcrumbs, then add the grated cheese and mustard powder (if using). Mix this through, pour in the milk and gently stir with your fingers to make a soft dough. Dust a work surface with extra flour, and also flour your rolling pin and hands. Gently roll out the dough until about 2cm thick, and using a small round pastry cutter or glass, cut out your scones. Place on a greased baking tray and bake in the middle of the oven for 10 minutes.

Reheat the soup and serve with buttered warm cheese scones.

Sam Hart
Fino, Fitzrovia, London

Joselito Ham Consommé

Joselito make some of the best jamón Iberico in Spain; however, if you cannot find Joselito bones, any Iberico ham bones or, failing that, jamón Serrano bones will suffice. Most good Spanish delicatessens will sell pre-sliced jamón bones.

1 carrot
1 bunch spring onions
2 onions
200ml dry sherry
1 bay leaf
1 clove
2.5kg Joselito ham bones, in pieces
a small handful of fresh parsley, finely chopped

Clarification
1 carrot
250g lean pork mince
1/2 leek
1/2 onion
4 egg whites
2 egg shells

Preheat the oven to 220ºC/Gas 7.

Finely chop the carrot, spring onions and onions and roast them, together with the ham bones, in the preheated oven until golden brown.

Add the sherry to the roasting pan, and deglaze until all the alcohol has evaporated.

Put all the soup ingredients apart from the parsley into a large saucepan, cover with water, bring to the boil, then simmer very gently for 2 1/2 hours.

Pass everything through a fine sieve into another saucepan, reserving the bones.

In a blender, blitz all the ingredients for the clarification process. Very slowly add the clarification mix into the soup. Simmer very slowly for 20 minutes. The clarification mix will have formed a crust on the top of the soup. Pour the liquid, very carefully, through a piece of muslin into a container, taking care not to break the crust. Keep pouring until you have poured

as much as you can from the saucepan, whilst leaving the crust behind. This liquid should be totally clear. You may wish to add/boil off some liquid at this point so as to achieve the desired concentration of flavour. Check the seasoning.

Rescue as much meat as possible from the roasted ham bones. Dice this finely and sprinkle into the consommé when you are ready to serve, along with a little finely chopped parsley.

Skye Gyngell

Petersham Nursery, Richmond, Surrey

Cauliflower Soup with Dolcelatte and Spiced Pear Relish

This is a beautiful autumn soup.

Serves 4

1 cauliflower
15g unsalted butter
2 shallots, finely sliced
1 garlic clove, finely chopped
4 sprigs fresh thyme
salt and pepper to taste
850ml Chicken Stock (see page 21)
200g dolcelatte cheese
120ml double cream

Spiced pear relish

25g unsalted butter
2 Conference (or any other ripe) pears, peeled and chopped into small chunks
1 Golden Delicious (you want an apple that will hold its shape), peeled and chopped into small chunks
75ml each of cider vinegar and cider
1 tbsp golden caster sugar
3 sprigs fresh lemon thyme

Trim the cauliflower, removing the outer leaves and stalks, so you are left with the florets.

Melt the butter over a gentle heat in a saucepan large enough to hold all the ingredients. Once the butter has melted, add the shallots and gently sweat until translucent. Now add the garlic, thyme and cauliflower. Cook, stirring occasionally, for a couple of minutes. Season with a little salt and (preferably white) pepper. Add the chicken stock, then place a lid on the saucepan and simmer gently for 10-15 minutes.

Meanwhile, make the relish. Melt the butter in a small pan. Add the apple and pears and allow to cook for 2-3 minutes over a gentle heat, until the fruit begins to soften. Add the remaining ingredients, and continue to cook, stirring frequently, for about a further 10 minutes. Taste and season with salt and pepper.

Crumble the dolcelatte into the soup, and add the cream, then purée in a blender. Return to the pan and taste to see if it needs extra seasoning. Add a little more salt and pepper – just enough to marry the flavours.

To serve, ladle the warm soup into soup bowls and put a tsp of pear relish in the centre.

Antony Worrall Thompson
Notting Grill, Notting Hill, London

Cauliflower and Potato Spice Soup

Serves 4

120g desiccated coconut, soaked in warm water
225g onions, thinly sliced
4 garlic cloves, finely chopped
75g unsalted butter
2 fresh red chillies, finely sliced
1 tsp coriander seeds
a pinch of mustard seeds
a pinch of fenugreek seeds (optional)
½ tsp cumin seeds
½ tsp ground black pepper

1 tsp powdered turmeric
1 tsp paprika
1 tsp grated fresh root ginger
225g potatoes, peeled and cubed
400ml Vegetable Stock (see page 19)
1 large cauliflower, cut into florets
1 x 400g can coconut milk
300ml double cream
salt and pepper to taste
coriander leaves for garnish

Squeeze the coconut dry and retain the soaking water. Set aside.

In a non-reactive saucepan, cook the onion and garlic gently in the butter until the onion has softened, about 6-8 minutes. Add the chillies, coriander, mustard and fenugreek seeds, the cumin seeds, black pepper, turmeric, paprika and ginger, and cook for 1 minute, stirring to combine.

Add the potatoes and reserved coconut, and cook until the potatoes start to stick to the bottom of the pan. Add the reserved coconut water and the stock. Cook until the potatoes are nearly tender. Add the cauliflower and coconut milk and cook for 12 minutes.

Ladle the soup into a liquidiser and blend until smooth. Pass through a fine sieve and return to the saucepan. If too thick, thin with extra stock.

Add the cream and season to taste, then heat through and serve garnished with coriander leaves.

Delia Smith

Food writer

Cauliflower Soup with Roquefort

This is a truly sublime soup, as the cauliflower and Roquefort seem to meld together so well, but I have also tried it with mature Cheddar and I'm sure it would be good with any cheese you happen to have handy. More good news – it takes little more than 40 minutes to make.

Serves 4-6

1 medium, good-sized cauliflower, about 570g
2 bay leaves
salt and pepper to taste
25g butter
1 medium onion, chopped
2 celery stalks, chopped
1 large leek, washed and chopped
110g potatoes, peeled and diced
2 tbsp half-fat crème fraîche
50g Roquefort cheese, crumbled, or mature

Cheddar, grated
1 tbsp snipped fresh chives

The stock for this is very simply made with all the cauliflower trimmings. All you do is trim the cauliflower into small florets and then take the stalk bits, including the green stems, and place these trimmings in a medium-sized saucepan. Then add 1.5 litres water, the bay leaves and some salt, bring it up to the boil and simmer for 20 minutes with a lid.

Meanwhile, take another large saucepan with a well-fitting lid. Melt the butter in it over a gentle heat, then add the onion, celery, leek and potato, cover and let the vegetables gently sweat for 15 minutes. Keep the heat very low, then when the stock is ready, strain it into the pan to join the vegetables, adding the bay leaves as well but throwing out the rest. Now add the cauliflower florets, bring it all back up to simmering point and simmer very gently for 20-25 minutes, until the cauliflower is completely tender, this time without a lid.

After that, remove the bay leaves, then place the contents of the saucepan in a food processor or blender and process until the soup is smooth and creamy. Next return it to the saucepan, stir in the crème fraîche and cheese, and keep stirring until the cheese has melted and the soup is hot but not boiling. Check the seasoning, then serve in hot bowls, garnished with the chives.

(© Delia Smith 1999. Recipe reproduced by permission from Delia Smith's *How to Cook*, BBC Worldwide)

Marcel Wanders
Dutch designer, originator of Can of Gold

Cauliflower Soup with Nutmeg Foam

This recipe was contributed by my good friend Peter Lute, who has a fantastic restaurant, Lute, in our home town, Amsterdam. He says that the best soups are the purest ones. I say the best ideas are the simplest.

Serves 4-6

2 litres water
600g cauliflower
30g salt
juice and rind of 1 lemon
1 blade of mace
salt and pepper to taste
400g whipping cream
freshly grated nutmeg

Put the water, cauliflower, salt and lemon juice into a large pan, and bring to the boil. Simmer for 10 minutes, then add the mace and 2 pieces of lemon rind. Leave to simmer for another 15 minutes.

Purée all the solid ingredients in a blender, then rub them through a fine sieve. Stir the purée through the liquid.

Taste the soup and season it with salt, pepper and, if you like, some more lemon juice.

Whip the whipping cream with nutmeg to taste and some salt and pepper.

Serve the soup as you would Irish coffee, with the cream on top.

Ruth Rogers and Rose Gray
River Café, Hammersmith, London

Chestnut and Celeriac Soup

This soup is one of the richest and most unusual. We first ate it in a restaurant in Liguria where there is an emphasis on seasonality and the use of vegetables and herbs in their simple menus.

Serves 6

60g unsalted butter
150g pancetta, finely sliced (5mm), then cut into pieces
4 small celeriac heads, peeled and cubed
2 inner white hearts of 2 heads celery, trimmed and roughly chopped
1 litre Chicken Stock to cover, barely (see page 21)
500g cooked and peeled chestnuts
2 garlic cloves, finely chopped
5 juniper berries, crushed

4 fresh bay leaves, centre spine removed, leaf part finely chopped
salt and pepper to taste
150ml double cream
100g Parmesan, freshly grated
extra virgin olive oil

In a large, thick-bottomed saucepan, melt the butter, add the pancetta and slow cook until transparent.

Add the celeriac and celery and stir to combine the flavours for a few minutes.

In a separate saucepan heat the chicken stock.

Add the whole peeled chestnuts and chopped garlic to the celeriac and celery. Cook on a low flame, stirring, then add the juniper berries and bay leaves.

Test the hot stock for seasoning, then pour in enough to just cover the vegetables. Bring to the boil and simmer for 15-20 minutes, or until the celeriac is soft.

Using a potato masher or wire whisk, break up the vegetables in the saucepan to achieve a rough, thick soup. Alternatively pulse-chop half the soup in a food processor, then return to the saucepan and combine.

Finally stir in the cream. Heat through and serve with grated Parmesan and a drizzle of extra virgin olive oil.

CASTANEA SATIVA

Angela Hartnett

The Connaught, Mayfair, London

Creamy Mushroom Soup

Serves 6

1kg flat mushrooms
2 large shallots, chopped
1 garlic clove, chopped
50g butter
1 litre Chicken Stock (see page 21)
500ml milk
100ml double cream
truffle oil to taste
salt and pepper to taste

Remove the gills from the mushrooms and chop the flesh up into quite large pieces. Sweat off the shallots and garlic in the butter until soft but before they have taken on any colour. Add the mushrooms and sweat down with the shallots and garlic.

Cover with the chicken stock and milk and simmer for about 20 minutes.

Blitz in a food processor, and pass through a sieve. Adjust the flavour and texture with the cream and extra milk if needed.

Season with truffle oil, salt and pepper, and serve with hot fresh bread (and some chopped parsley if you like).

Tom Conran
Restaurateur

White Bean and Carrot Soup

This is extremely heartening and comforting.

Serves 4

**500g haricot beans, soaked for 3-4 hours
and drained**
1 small bunch parsley
4 garlic cloves, peeled
1 ripe tomato, halved
500g carrots, peeled and finely sliced
3 tbsp extra virgin olive oil
1.25 litres Chicken Stock (see page 21)
salt and pepper to taste
**4 thin slices toasted sourdough, rye or
country-style bread**

Boil the soaked beans in plenty of fresh unsalted water with the parsley stalks (keep the leaves), 2 of the garlic cloves, crushed, and the tomato halves, until the beans are al dente, about 30-45 minutes. Drain.

Coarsely chop the remaining garlic and fry with the carrots in 2 tbsp of the olive oil for 2-3 minutes over a medium high heat, stirring occasionally. Add the cooked beans, chicken stock and the coarsely chopped parsley leaves, and simmer for 20 minutes.

Remove half the beans and purée them, then return them to the pot, stir to mix and season with sea salt and cracked black pepper.

Grill the bread and put one slice in the bottom of each bowl. Drizzle over the remaining olive oil, season with sea salt, and spoon over the hot soup.

Pascal Aussignac

Club Gascon, Clerkenwell, London

Watercress Velouté, Grilled Mussels and Chestnuts

Bon appetit!

Serves 6

2kg fresh mussels
100ml extra virgin olive oil
2 bunches watercress
salt and pepper to taste
1 floury potato, peeled and diced
50g unsalted butter
250g cooked and peeled chestnuts, thinly sliced

Clean the mussels. Wash in running water and strain them. Take a large saucepan with a lid and heat it at a high temperature on the stove. Pour the mussels into the saucepan and add a splash of olive oil. Cover with the lid for 2 minutes until the mussels are just open. Discard any that fail to open. Reserve the mussels in a large bowl, sieve the juice and reserve. Once the mussels have cooled down, clean them further by taking off the beards.

Wash the watercress. Boil some water in a saucepan with a pinch of salt. Add the watercress and cook it at boiling point for 7 minutes. Stop the cooking process by plunging the watercress into very cold water (add ice cubes for best results).

Put the reserved mussel juice keeping 1 tbsp aside in a small saucepan, add the potato dice, and cook until melting.

Mix the watercress up little by little, in the blender, with the remaining mussel juice until it forms a perfectly smooth texture. Add the cooked potato, the remaining olive oil and seasoning, and finish blending.

Reheat the velouté and add most of the butter. In a frying pan, sauté the mussels for a few seconds on one side in the remaining butter.

Pour the velouté into the plates and top it with the mussels and the cut chestnuts.

Nico Ladenis
Deca, Mayfair, London

Mussel Soup with Saffron

Serves 6

120g butter
2 tbsp olive oil
½ onion, finely diced
1 carrot, finely diced
½ leek, washed and finely diced
1 small bunch fresh parsley
4 garlic cloves, finely chopped
2 sprigs fresh tarragon
salt and pepper to taste
1 litre mussels

1 bottle dry white wine
400ml double cream
1 small sachet saffron
1 tbsp finely chopped fresh chive

Melt the butter with the olive oil in a large frying pan and sauté the diced vegetables until soft. Add the parsley, garlic and tarragon with a little salt and plenty of pepper, and cook for a further couple of minutes, stirring well. Remove from the heat.

Scrape the mussels well and make sure that they are very clean. Discard any that gape and do not close when tapped (they are dead). Pour the wine into a large saucepan and throw in the mussels. Cook until they open, then leave to cool.

When cool, strain, reserving the liquid, and remove the mussels from their shells. Pass the mussel liquid through several layers of muslin, making sure that all the sediment is discarded. Set aside some of the best mussels.

Place the remaining mussels in the pan with the vegetables. Pour in the strained wine and simmer for 20 minutes. Tip into a chinois, and press well to extract all the juices.

Return the liquid to a clean pan, add the cream, bring to the boil, then add the saffron. Simmer for a few minutes, stirring well, and skim off any scum which may rise to the surface.

Add the reserved mussels and sprinkle with chives. Serve. Enjoy.

Steve Evenett-Watts
Villandry, Fitzrovia, London

Chicken, Spinach and Shiitake Mushroom Soup

For me a good simple soup is a perfect dish on its own, a complete meal in itself, and yet because of this I think it can be one of the most difficult things to cook. As well as a good recipe, when making soup you also need an extra touch, an extra dash of creativity.

Serves 6

3 carrots, diced
3 celery stalks, diced
1 onion, diced
2 tbsp olive oil
2 garlic cloves, chopped
180g shiitake mushrooms, sliced
a handful of young spinach leaves
freshly grated nutmeg
salt and pepper to taste

Make the stock first. Put all the ingredients into a medium pot, cover with water – about 2.5 litres – and bring to the boil. Skim the scum that floats to the surface, and gently simmer the stock until the chicken has cooked, about 1½ hours. Leave the chicken to cool in the stock.

Sweat the diced carrot, celery and onion in the oil in a medium pan together with the garlic until the vegetables are soft. Add the sliced shiitake mushrooms and gently fry until cooked.

When the stock is ready, strain the liquid over the vegetables and mushrooms. You need 2 litres.

Keep the chicken carcass and pick off the cooked meat in small chunks. Add this to the soup with a handful of washed spinach. When the spinach has wilted in the soup, add some grated nutmeg, season with salt and pepper, and serve.

Chicken stock
1 boiling fowl
1 onion, roughly chopped
2 carrots, roughly chopped
3 celery stalks, roughly chopped
2 bay leaves

If you fancy, you could add a poached egg or some grated Parmesan on top for a change.

Terence Conran
Restaurateur

Borscht

We opened The Soup Kitchen in 1953 in Chandos Place, just off Trafalgar Square, offering four different soups made from a base of our own very good stock. The doors opened to 42 tramps and one journalist. They got their meal free and we got some very good publicity.

Beetroot never fails to amaze – that the depth and intensity of its colour is achieved in the garden is one of nature's miracles. Borscht, one of Russia's better-known culinary exports, is the classic beetroot soup. The earthy flavour is complemented by a good rich beef stock. Served hot in the winter, it is equally good chilled as a summer soup. Whatever, the colour is ravishing and demands the purest white soup plates.

Serves 4-6

50g butter
250g raw beetroot, peeled and roughly chopped
1 onion, chopped
1 carrot, chopped
3 garlic cloves, chopped
1 tbsp caster sugar
1.5 litres Beef Stock (see page 20)
salt and pepper to taste
juice of ½ lemon

To garnish
soured cream
a handful of chopped chives

Melt the butter in a large pan, over a gentle heat and slowly sweat the beetroot, onion, carrot and garlic, turning the vegetables (which will become a lurid pink) over in the butter.

Add the sugar and stock to the pan, season with a few grinds of pepper, bring the soup to a simmer and cook for about 40 minutes until the vegetables are tender.

Using a blender, whizz the soup until it is entirely smooth, then add the lemon juice and salt to taste. A swirl of soured cream and a scattering of chopped chives is the traditional garnish – delicious, and adding another dimension to the fabulous beetroot colour.

(From *Classic Conran, Plain, Simple and Satisfying Food*, Terence and Vicki Conran, Conran Octopus, 2003)

Winter

Scallops, Pears, Carrots, Turnips, Goose, Leeks, Squash, Cabbage, Parsnip, Shallots, Lobster, Forced Rhubarb, Celeriac, Halibut, Guinea Fowl, Mussels, Chicory, Cockles, Purple Sprouting Broccoli, Sugar-snap Peas, Pomegranates.

Andrew Turner

1880, South Kensington, London

Curried Mussels, Tomato, Coriander and Fennel

Serves 10

4kg Dutch mussels, washed and prepared
3 tbsp olive oil
2 onions, diced
2 celery stalks
2 leeks, washed, the white parts diced
50g unsalted butter
2 tsp garam masala
2 pinches saffron strands
½ tsp cayenne pepper

300ml dry white wine
3 litres Fish Stock (see page 23)
1 litre whipping cream
salt and pepper to taste

To serve
6 vine tomatoes
3 fennel bulbs
⅛ bunch fresh coriander, chopped

Put the mussels in a pan with the hot olive oil, the vegetables and butter. Cook for 5 minutes or until the mussels have opened, and then drain them off (discard any that do not open). Return the liquid to the stove and add the garam masala, saffron, cayenne pepper and deglaze with the white wine. Boil to reduce by half, then add the fish stock and the whipping cream and cook out to soup consistency. Adjust seasoning as necessary.

Meanwhile, pick the mussels from their shells while they are still warm and keep for the garnish. Do not allow the mussels to be exposed to the air as they dry and discolour quickly.

Halve the tomatoes, and seed. Cut into 3cm squares. Trim and slice the fennel, and cut into similar sized squares. Cook these in a little oil.

Garnish each plate with squares of tomato and cooked fennel. Place a small amount of the mussels in the centre, and top with coriander.

Jamie Thewes

Port-na-Craig, Pitlochry, Perthshire

Lightly Curried Mussel Broth with Turmeric

From the Gulf of Mexico a warm, rich current sweeps its way across the Atlantic. Billions of nutrients from the seas off Florida and Mexico are carried north-west, bringing life in abundance. This massive stream of water brushes against the coast of Scotland before dispersing in the Arctic. Its effect on the west coast is phenomenal, supporting a vast biodiversity both in the sea and on the land.

One beneficiary is the mussel, which thrives in this environment. Although mussel farming is said to have started in 12th-century France, it only became a real commercial industry in Scotland about 30 years ago. It now accounts for some 75 per cent of shellfish production in Britain. Being sheltered, sea lochs provide a perfect place for mussel farms. Mussels are grown on ropes suspended from rafts. Juveniles attach themselves naturally and grow there feeding on plankton just as they do in the wild, until they are harvested two years later. The advantage of these rope-grown mussels is that they are clean, with no sand or grit as with many found naturally.

Mussels are available all year round, and don't have a season as such. They are, however, at their best in winter in the run-up to spawning. We're very lucky to have such an abundance of this wonderful creature. Not only does it have valuable nutritional properties, being high in calcium, iron and iodine, but it's incredibly versatile and delicious. There are two things to watch out for though – any that won't shut before cooking and any that won't open after cooking must be thrown away.

Serves 4

1.5kg live mussels
250ml dry white wine
1 onion, chopped
1 dsp coriander seeds
1 small hot fresh chilli, diced
1 cinnamon stick
2 star anise pods

2 bay leaves
10 black peppercorns
3 garlic cloves, roughly chopped
a small pinch of saffron threads
olive oil or ghee
1 tbsp ground turmeric
150ml coconut milk

Clean the mussels, and discard any that won't shut. Simmer the wine with the onion, coriander, chilli, cinnamon, star anise, bay leaves, peppercorns, garlic and saffron in a pot with a tightly fitting lid for 4 minutes, to release the flavours into the stock.

Add the mussels, turn up the heat and replace the lid. Shake the pot after about a minute then remove the lid and have a look. If all the mussels haven't opened, carry on for another minute or two.

When all the mussels have opened remove the pot from the heat and pour the liquid through a fine sieve into a bowl. Remove one shell from each mussel.

Put 1 tbsp olive oil or ghee into a clean pot and gently fry the turmeric for a minute. Slowly whisk in the coconut milk followed by the mussel stock. Replace the mussels, warm them through and serve with warm naan bread.

Rowley Leigh

Kensington Place, Notting Hill, London

Bacon, Chestnut and Potato Soup with Rosemary

Serves 4

750g chestnuts
50g butter
250g bacon, cut into small cubes
1 onion
3 celery stalks
2 garlic cloves
salt and pepper to taste
3 sprigs fresh thyme
1 sprig fresh rosemary

1 litre Chicken Stock (see page 21, or use a cube)
300g peeled potato
extra virgin olive oil

Preheat the oven to 220ºC/Gas 7. With a small sharp knife, cut a small incision in each chestnut and place them in an oven tray. Roast the chestnuts for 20 minutes or until the skins burst. Allow to cool before peeling, removing the inner skin at the same time.

Melt the butter in a heavy saucepan and add the bacon, cooking it over a medium heat so that it slowly browns and renders its fat. Chop the onion, celery and garlic into small dice and add to the bacon, letting them stew gently together for 15 minutes. Season well with pepper – no salt for the moment – then add the herbs and the stock and bring gently to the boil.

Chop the potato into neat small dice and add to the soup. Chop the chestnuts quite small also and simmer them all together in the pot for 20 minutes. Season with salt and pepper as required and serve, again with a spoonful of good extra virgin olive oil poured on top if desired.

Camilla Schneiderman
Divertimenti, Marylebone, London

Spiced Roasted Parsnip Soup

This soup proved very popular at a recent cookery class. No need for gentle sweating of onions, instead the vegetables are roasted in a delicate spice mix and then blended with stock. Simple but surprisingly delicious..

Serves 4

4 medium parsnips, peeled and cut into 1cm dice
2 medium carrots, peeled and cut into 1 cm dice
1 medium or 2 small onions, cut roughly into 8 pieces
4 medium tomatoes, cut roughly into 8 pieces
3 garlic cloves
3 tbsp olive oil
1 tsp coriander seeds
1/2 tsp black mustard seeds
1 tsp ground cumin

1/2 tsp powdered turmeric
salt and pepper to taste
750ml Vegetable or Chicken Stock (see pages 19 or 21)
juice of 1/2 lemon
a handful of roughly chopped fresh parsley

Preheat the oven to 180ºC/Gas 4.

Place all the vegetables, including the garlic, in a large bowl. Add the olive oil, spices and seasoning and mix thoroughly.

Transfer to a baking tray and roast in the preheated oven until the vegetables are soft and beginning to brown.

When cooked, place the roasted vegetables in the bowl of a food processor and blend thoroughly, adding hot stock through the spout until the desired consistency is reached. Taste and adjust the seasoning if necessary.

Serve the soup piping hot with a squeeze of lemon juice and a sprinkling of chopped parsley.

Shirley Spear
Three Chimneys, Colbost, Isle of Skye

Oatmeal and Potato Soup

I was once asked by a Scottish radio programme to prepare some hearty soup recipes to cheer up the nation, as Scotland had been suffering from an epidemic of winter colds and flu. This soup is simple to make and uses traditional Scottish ingredients that take me 'back to the basics' of nourishing home cooking. It was very well received by the radio listeners and the programme received its biggest ever postbag requesting a copy of the recipe! It is popular in the restaurant for lunch on a cold day and my family love it too. As a special treat, serve with freshly baked wholemeal bread, or wholemeal cheese scones, warm from the oven.

Serves 6-8 (generously)

50g Scottish butter
300g peeled and finely chopped onion
600g peeled and diced potatoes (choose a floury potato which is good for mash)
salt and pepper to taste
1 generous litre Vegetable or Chicken Stock (see pages 19 or 21)
2 rounded tbsp medium oatmeal
approx. 300ml fresh milk
200ml double cream

freshly grated nutmeg
chopped fresh chives, to garnish

Melt the butter in a large saucepan until foamy. Add the onion, turn in the butter and cook until softened. Add the potatoes, and stir together with the onion. Add a sprinkling of salt and some freshly ground black pepper. Allow to cook gently for a few minutes. Pour in the stock, bring to the boil and then simmer with the lid on for at least 20-30 minutes.

Add the oatmeal, stir and simmer for a further 10 minutes. Add the milk and liquidise.

Reheat and finish with cream, more seasoning if necessary and some freshly grated nutmeg. If too thick, add a little more milk or cream. Serve immediately, as the longer this soup is left to stand, the thicker it becomes because of the oatmeal. Sprinkle with freshly chopped chives.

If using chicken stock and adding cooked chicken pieces at the end, make sure the soup is heated thoroughly. Add some finely chopped leeks with the chopped onion, at the beginning, for a further variation.

Antonio Carluccio
Restaurateur and Food Writer

Cabbage Soup, Valtellina Style
Zuppa di Cavolo Valtellinense

What a wonderful (and economical) way of using leftover bread. Cabbage is cheap, too. The other ingredients are very typical of the Aosta Valley and make this remarkable, simple and delicious winter dish. Mmmmm.

Serves 4

675g Savoy cabbage
salt and pepper to taste
6 slices stale bread, cut into cubes
275g Fontina cheese, cut into small cubes
1 litre Chicken Stock (see page 21)
50g butter

Clean, trim and slice the cabbage. Boil in lightly salted water until tender, then drain. Place a large saucepan over a low heat. Put a layer of cabbage while still warm in the bottom, then a layer of bread, then a layer of Fontina cheese.

Continue doing this until the ingredients are finished. Gently press down the ingredients with the ladle. Bring the stock to the boil and pour over the other ingredients. Leave to soak for a couple of minutes.

Meanwhile, melt the butter in a small pan. While still foaming pour it over the soup. Stir and serve hot.

(From *Antonio Carluccio's Italian Feast*, BBC Books, 1996)

Germain Schwab

Winteringham Fields, Winteringham, Lincolnshire

Consommé of Wood Pigeon with Beetroot Foam

A good soup reflects the seasons and the produce from the countryside around you, wholesome and comforting... A just reward at the end of a hard day. To make the beetroot foam you will need a cream-making siphon. These are available from all good kitchen shops – Habitat, Cucina Direct etc. – and are brilliant for making cream foam on puddings. We like to use them for savoury dishes too, like this soup!!

Serves 6

6 wood pigeons
3 tbsp vegetable oil
2 large carrots, finely diced
1 celery stalk, finely diced
1 large white onion, finely diced
6 garlic cloves, crushed
1 leek, washed and finely diced
300g beetroot, peeled and finely diced
1 bay leaf
3 cloves

1 bunch fresh thyme
500ml red wine
100ml sweet sherry
1.5 litres water
salt and white pepper to taste
160ml double cream

Remove the pigeon breast fillets from the carcasses and put to one side. Crush the legs and carcass with a chopping knife on a chopping board.

In a heavy-based pan, brown the legs and carcasses in a little oil. Once nicely coloured, add the finely diced vegetables plus half of the beetroot, and sweat all the ingredients for a further 10-15 minutes. Add the bay leaves, cloves and thyme. Deglaze the pan with the wine and sherry, add the water and bring to the boil. Turn the heat down, and simmer for 1½ hours to reduce the liquid.

Pass the liquid through muslin, adding seasoning to taste. Reduce the liquid further if necessary.

To make the beetroot foam, bring the rest of the beetroot to the boil in salted water until very soft. Drain off the water and peel off the skin. Place the beetroot in a liquidiser with 400ml of the pigeon broth and blend until smooth. Pass the liquid through 4 layers of muslin. Boil the double cream for 1½ minutes, add this to the beetroot liquid, and pour into the siphon.

Pan-fry the small fillets of pigeon for about 30-35 seconds on each side in the remaining oil, depending on the size of the pigeon breasts. Leave to rest whilst still keeping them warm for about 2 minutes. Slice each breast in half and place 2 halves in each soup plate. Pour in some of the pigeon broth.

Add the gas cartridge to the cream siphon, and pipe a little of the foam on top of the pigeon broth in the centre of the soup dish. Serve.

Martin Burge

Whatley Manor, Easton Grey, Wiltshire

Chilled Celeriac Consommé with Lightly Smoked Duck

I love soups, I think they are brilliant and rather understated. This recipe is one of my very own creations, and is very versatile, as it can be served both hot and cold and enjoyed just as much in the winter as the summer!

Serves 4

Consommé (makes 600ml)
2.25kg celeriac

Clarification
130g celery, diced
100g egg whites
10g celery leaves
7g salt

Beetroot garnish
120g beetroot

200ml apple juice
a pinch of salt
3 turns white pepper

Smoked duck garnish
2 Gressingham duck breasts (420g approx.)
8g rock salt
2g cracked black pepper
7g dried orange zest
1.5g star anise
55g brown sugar

To start the consommé, wash and peel the outside layer from the celeriac. Cut the celeriac into even pieces so they can be placed into a juicer. Extract the juice and put in a medium saucepan.

Add the clarification ingredients to the celeriac juice, and bring up to a gentle simmer to form a crust (this should take approximately 15 minutes). Pass through fine muslin to separate the crust from the consommé. Place the consommé in the fridge to become very cold.

To prepare the beetroot garnish, peel and cut the beetroot into 1cm dice. Place the apple juice, salt, pepper and diced beetroot in a pan and cook below a simmer for approximately 3 hours. Allow the beetroot time to cool down in the apple juice, then refrigerate.

To prepare the smoked duck garnish, have ready a smoker. Trim any excess fat and unwanted sinew from the duck breasts. Add the rock salt and cracked pepper and marinate for 1 hour. Rub the seasoning off. Heat a pan to medium hot, and add the duck breast to render the fat and to crisp up the skin, approximately 5 minutes before the skin is golden brown.

Add the dried orange zest, star anise and brown sugar to the smoker then place the duck breast on the rack, cover with a tight-fitting lid, and smoke for approximately 10 minutes until the duck is just cooked pink. Allow 20 minutes for the duck to cool down to room temperature before serving.

To serve, thinly slice the duck breasts at an angle. Place some duck breast and beetroot in each bowl. Pour the consommé on to the garnishes and serve.

Nigella Lawson
Food writer

Yellow Split Pea and Frankfurter Soup

The glorious golden yellowness of the soup makes it a suitable marker for the New Year, implying, as it does, a hope for golden times ahead. I felt, too, the split peas themselves were a kind of northern European take on the Italian custom of serving lentils for their coin-like appearance.

But the value of this soup is so much more than symbolic, important though that is in festive eating particularly. The grainy liquid is hearty on its own, and the best way of soaking up excess alcohol – or after-effects of same – lingering in the system. The frankfurters, again to be sliced in coins if you want to play further on this theme, or cut in thick slices otherwise, make this a real meal and a half.

Serves 6-8

1 onion
1 carrot
1 garlic clove
1 celery stalk
2-3 tbsp vegetable oil
½ tsp ground mace
500g yellow split peas
1.25-1.5 litres Chicken or Vegetable Stock (see pages 21 or 19)

2 bay leaves
approx. 8 frankfurters

Peel the onion, carrot and garlic and cut the onion and carrot into rough chunks. Put them all, along with the roughly cut-up celery, into the bowl of a food processor. Blitz until all are finely chopped.

Spoon the oil into a heavy-based wide saucepan and put on a medium heat. When warm, add the chopped vegetables from the processor and cook for 5-10 minutes, until soft but not coloured.

Add the ground mace – this may be a small amount but it's crucial to the taste – give a good stir and then add the split peas and stir again till they're glossily mixed with the oil-slicked, cooked-down vegetables. Pour over 1.25 litres stock and add the bay leaves, then bring to the boil. Cover, turn down the heat and cook for about an hour until everything is tender and

sludgy, adding more stock as needed. Sometimes the peas seem to thicken too much before they actually cook and need to be watered down. Taste for seasoning once everything's ready.

You can add the frankfurters as you wish. It's probably easiest just to cut them into slices – I tend to add them in chunks of about 3cm each – and throw them into the soup to warm, but I just put them into the microwave (40 seconds on high is about right for one or two franks; fiddle about with times when there are more), then slice them hot and add them to each person's bowl as they come. Not an elegant soup, I'll admit, but a near-perfect one.

(From *Feast*, Nigella Lawson, Chatto & Windus, 2004)

John Campbell
Vineyard at Stockcross, Berkshire

Red Lentil Soup

This is my grandmother's recipe for red lentil soup that was served to me as a child every Saturday morning in the winter. The recipe means a great deal to me as my grandmother was less than well off, and this soup was a by-product of cooking the Sunday boiled ham/joint. The stock from this on the Saturday morning was then transferred.

Serves 4-6

100ml olive oil
3 baby shallots, finely diced
½ celery stalk, finely diced
½ leek, washed and finely diced
500g red lentils, soaked overnight and drained

1 carrot
1 bay leaf
2 garlic cloves, halved
2 cloves
8 white peppercorns

Ham stock
1 medium ham hock
4 litres cold water
½ onion

For the ham stock, place the ham hock in a pan and cover with water. Add the onion, carrot, herbs and spices, and bring to the boil. Turn the heat down to a slow simmer, and cook for about 3 hours. When the hock is cooked, the centre bone will slide out in one smooth motion. Drain, reserving both meat and broth. Eat the ham separately.

For the soup, heat the oil in a suitable pan. Add the diced vegetables and cook until they are slightly coloured. Add the drained lentils, then pour in enough of your ham stock to cover them. Bring to the boil, then turn the heat down to a very slow simmer. Cook until all the lentils have broken down, about 50 minutes, but start checking after 40 minutes.

Allow to cool for 10 minutes, and then purée until nice and smooth. It may be necessary to alter the consistency of the soup by using cream, milk or water – whatever you prefer.

Charles Campion
Food and restaurant writer

Pheasants in Jerusalem

Soup is real food. Think cosy kitchens, deep bowls, crusty bread - but that's no reason it should end up lumpen. I am a big fan of thinning vegetable purée soups with skimmed milk rather than stock, you get a lighter, jollier soup that way. Many vegetable soups also benefit from having some lumps of meat floating around in them!

Serves 4

50g unsalted butter
2 pheasant breasts, skinned
200g English onions, finely chopped
500g Jerusalem artichokes, peeled and finely sliced
a fat pinch of ground mace
up to 1 litre skimmed milk
salt and pepper to taste

Melt the butter in a frying pan and cook the pheasant breasts gently until they are done, about 12-15 minutes. Lift out the pheasant and put on one side, leaving the butter in the pan.

Add the onions, artichokes and a fat pinch of ground mace to the pan. Then sweat the vegetables until they are very soft but not brown, about 20-25 minutes.

Put the soggy veg into a deep saucepan, and liquidise with a hand-held blender. (Or use a free-standing blender or processor, and pour the purée back into a deep saucepan.)

Thin the purée down with some of the skimmed milk. Stop adding milk when the soup is as thick or as thin as you want it to be. Season well with salt and pepper.

Slice the cooked pheasant breasts into chunks, and add them to the soup.

Reheat and adjust the seasoning. Serve with pride.

Anna Hansen

Providores, Mayfair, London

Spicy Beetroot, Celeriac, Kombu and Miso Broth with Edamame, Shiitake and Creamy Yuzu Tofu

The beauty of this delicious and refreshing, vitamin- and mineral-rich soup is the ease with which it is prepared. I prefer to use white miso but if you cannot find this you may use any other type of miso, just beware that they may be saltier so add a little at a time to taste.

Serves 6

500g beetroot, peeled and chopped
650g celeriac, peeled and chopped
350g fennel bulb, chopped
15cm piece kombu
1 onion, quartered
2 garlic cloves
6 stalks flat-leaf parsley
30g dried shiitake mushrooms
1.5 litres Vegetable Stock (see page 19)
6 stalks coriander, leaves picked and stems reserved
2 tsp white miso
1½ tsp shichimi (seven-spice seasoning)

juice of ½ lemon
200g fresh shiitake mushrooms, destalked and sliced
300ml toasted sesame oil
150g steamed and podded edamame beans
4 spring onions, finely sliced

Tofu purée
120g firm tofu
1 tbsp yuzu
2 tsp soy sauce
1 tbsp sesame seeds

Combine all the ingredients from the beetroot through to the vegetable stock in a large saucepan, add the picked coriander stalks, and gently simmer for 45 minutes. If there is not enough liquid to cover the vegetables, add some water.

Strain into another pot and add the miso and shichimi. For more heat, add more shichimi but be wary, it is powerful stuff! Add the lemon juice to taste and adjust the seasoning by adding a little more miso if needed. (If you find the miso flavour is sufficient but the broth needs more seasoning, add a little salt.)

For the tofu purée, put the tofu, yuzu and soy sauce in a food processor and blitz. Transfer the purée to a bowl and stir in the sesame seeds.

Fry the fresh shiitakes in a little sesame oil then remove from the pan and divide them and the edamame between 6 bowls. Pour over the broth, dollop in some tofu purée then add the coriander leaves and spring onions. Serve immediately.

Note
Kombu is a sea vegetable often referred to as kelp. It is sold in health food stores and some Asian shops. Yuzu is a Japanese citrus fruit used almost exclusively for its aromatic rind.

Faith MacArthur
Founder of EAT

EAT – Hungarian Goulash

Hungry and cold on the ramparts of the Hohensalzburg Fortress in Salzburg with my husband on a snowy winter's evening in 1989, talking too loudly in English about a hot meal, preferably of goulash, we were accosted by a smartly dressed couple who invited us – without preamble – to come to their home and...eat goulash!

So off we went to enjoy the wonderful hospitality of this generous, food-loving couple in their warm Salzburg kitchen. Perfect!

Traditional goulash, it transpired, is made without any water at all. Equal amounts of onion and beef left to simmer will generate all the liquid required for this dish. The simplicity impressed us and we resolved, some seven years later when we started EAT, to make a Hungarian goulash soup along the same lines. Adding some stock to attain the consistency needed for soup felt rather blasphemous but it works and we love this recipe – as do our customers.

EAT is a small company dedicated to quality food. We believe in simplicity, honesty and using real ingredients – hence our name The Real Food Company. Our soups are all cooked in our own kitchen to our own recipes much as you would at home, with lots of chopping, dicing, stirring and simmering.

We love fresh, delicious hot soup and are constantly inspired by people like our Salzburg friends with a passion for food.

Serves 6

700g beef chuck steak, cut into 2.5cm (1in) cubes
700g onions (about 5), diced
2 tbsp olive oil
2 heaped tbsp sweet Hungarian paprika
½ tsp whole caraway seeds
250g tomatoes, chopped
750ml Beef Stock (see page 20)
3 large potatoes, peeled and cut into large dice
salt and pepper to taste
chopped fresh flat-leaf parsley

Heat the oil over high heat (best in a heavy cast-iron pot). Sear the chuck steak in small batches to ensure a nice rich colour and then set aside.

In the same pot sauté the diced onions in the olive oil, stirring until they begin to colour, then lower the heat and cover, letting them sweat until soft.

When the onions are soft, add the paprika, caraway, tomato, seared beef and beef stock. Cover and let simmer for at least an hour until the meat becomes very tender. Add the cubed potatoes and cook another half-hour until tender. Season with salt and pepper to taste.

Serve nice and hot with a sprinkling of chopped parsley.

Ainsley Harriott
Food writer

Sweet Potato, Chickpea and Spinach Soup

This is a hearty and warming soup - a lovely one for vegetarian friends. Add some crusty bread and it makes quite a substantial supper.

Serves 4

2 tbsp olive oil
1 onion, finely chopped
1 large sweet potato, peeled and diced
1 garlic clove, thinly sliced
1 tsp cumin seeds
1 x 400g can chickpeas, drained
2 tomatoes, roughly chopped
1 tsp honey
1 tbsp dijon mustard

900ml hot Vegetable Stock (see page 19)
225g baby leaf spinach
salt and pepper to taste

Heat the oil in a large pan and cook the onion, sweet potato and garlic for 5 minutes, stirring until golden brown. Add the cumin seeds and cook for 30 seconds. Stir in the chickpeas, tomatoes, honey and mustard, and cook for 1-2 minutes, until the tomatoes begin to soften.

Stir in the hot stock and bring to the boil, then cover and simmer for 10 minutes until the sweet potato is tender.

Stir in the baby leaf spinach and cook for a further minute, stirring all the while until the spinach wilts. Season to taste and serve.

Richard Learoyd
Photographer, Soup Kitchen

Clear Soup with Sea Bass

This soup, a Japanese delicacy, was written for me by my friend Yuko Tanaka, who is from Tokyo and writes Japanese cookery books. Her boyfriend's studio is right by mine. I love the way that the Japanese can make water taste interesting by putting all these things in it. I like the way the bits float to the top and you can chase them around with your spoon.

Serves 4

20g kombu (dried kelp – see page 86)
about 1 litre water
15g katsuo-bushi (dried Japanese fish flakes)
2 types of mushroom, maybe 2 large flat mushrooms, sliced, and 4 small button mushrooms, halved
a little bit of fresh root ginger, peel off
4 large spring onions, cut into lengths of 3cm or so

4 sea bass fillets, scaled, each cut into 2-3 pieces, scored
1 tsp soy sauce

To serve
finely chopped spring onion or fresh chive and ginger
2 limes or sudachi (Japanese limes)

Wipe the piece of kombu gently (or sometimes it comes in several small pieces) with a damp cloth and soak it in the water in the pan which you are going to use to make the soup. Leave it to soak for 5-10 minutes if you have time.

Heat it for about 10 minutes, uncovered, on a medium heat. Take out the kombu just before the water boils. If you boil the water with the kombu in it, you will lose most of the flavour. (You can get an even richer, more delicate flavour by soaking the kombu in cold water for 8 hours instead of heating it in the pan.)

Now with the kombu removed, gently boil the water. Add a dash of cold water (50ml or so) to bring the temperature down. Now immediately add the fish flakes. No stirring is required, just bring to the boil and then immediately remove from the heat, which will only take a couple of minutes. (If the fish flakes are boiled for more than a few seconds, the soup will lose its delicate taste and become overly fishy in flavour.) Let the soup stand until all the flakes have sunk to the bottom of the pan (about 1 minute), then remove any froth from the surface with a small sieving spoon. Strain the soup gently into a jug or bowl and rinse out the pan.

Now put the stock back into the pan and heat gently. Add the mushrooms and ginger. Once the mushrooms start to become tender, add the chopped spring onion and pieces of sea bass. It will not take more than 5 minutes for the sea bass to cook. Add soy sauce as a final touch of flavour just before removing the pan from the heat.

Pour the soup into bowls and sprinkle with some finely chopped spring onions, chives or ginger as a garnish. Serve half a lime with each bowl and ask your guests to squeeze it over their soup. Enjoy!

Darina Allen
Ballymaloe Cookery School, Co. Cork

Irish Colcannon Soup

Soup is something so warm, comforting and nostalgic: warm and bubbly, warming your hands as you retreat from the cold; reviving when tired; restorative when ill. If you have soup in the fridge or freezer you will never be short of something to eat. Colcannon is one of Ireland's best-loved traditional potato dishes, fluffy mashed potato flecked with cooked cabbage or kale. This recipe uses identical ingredients to make a delicious soup.

Serves 6

55g butter
450g potatoes, peeled and diced
120g onions, diced
salt and pepper to taste
1.1 litre Chicken or Vegetable Stock (see pages 21 and 19)
130ml creamy milk

Buttered cabbage
450g Savoy cabbage
40g butter

Melt the butter in a heavy-bottomed saucepan. When it foams, add the potato and onion and toss in the butter until well coated. Season with salt and pepper. Cover and sweat on a gentle heat for 6-10 minutes. Add the stock, increase the heat, and cook until the vegetables are soft but not coloured.

Meanwhile make the buttered cabbage. Remove the tough outer leaves from the cabbage. Divide into four, cut out the stalks and then cut into fine shreds across the grain. Put 2-3 tbsp water into a wide saucepan with half the butter and a pinch of salt. Bring to the boil, add the cabbage and toss constantly over a high heat, then cover for a few minutes. Toss again and add some more salt, pepper and the remaining butter.

Purée the potato and onion mixture in a blender or food processor, and return to a clean pan. Add the cabbage to the soup. Taste and adjust seasoning. Thin with creamy milk to the required consistency.

Note
The cabbage may be puréed with the soup if a smoother texture is your preference.

Roz Denny
Food Writer

Pizzoccheri Soup

This soup is based on a great Italian Alps pasta and vegetable dish. It's more of a main meal than starter, and delicious after a hard day's ski-ing! Season the soup lightly during cooking, then serve sprinkled with Maldon salt.

In these salt conscious days, it makes sense to choose the best salt to enhance the natural flavour of your food. I love the purity of Maldon salt and the hint of sweetness when it melts on the tongue. But most of all I love crushing the pure flaky crystals into dishes as I cook.

Serves 4

1 large potato, about 350g, peeled and chopped
1 onion, chopped
3 fat garlic cloves, chopped
4 tbsp olive oil
1.5 litres Vegetable Stock (see page 19, but can be made with a cube)
salt and pepper to taste
100g buckwheat or wholewheat spaghetti, broken
100g green cabbage, shredded
75g Bitto or Fontina cheese, cubed
Maldon sea salt

Put the potato, onion, garlic and oil in a large saucepan. Sauté gently for 5 minutes until softened.

Pour in the stock, season lightly, bring to the boil and simmer, partially covered, for 10-12 minutes until the potato softens. Add the broken pasta and cook for another 5 minutes, then mix in the cabbage. Return to a simmer for another 5 minutes.

Mix in the cheese cubes and ladle into warmed soup bowls. Serve with pinches of crushed Maldon sea salt on top.

Daniel Woodhouse

McClement's Restaurant, Twickenham, London

Jerusalem Artichoke and Oyster Soup

Serves 8

125g butter
2 large banana shallots, or 4 round shallots,
finely chopped
2 garlic cloves, finely chopped
800g Jerusalem artichokes, peeled and
chopped
1 bunch fresh thyme, chopped
2 bay leaves
1 litre Fish Stock (see page 23)
500ml double cream

20 native oysters, shucked, retaining their liquor
salt and pepper to taste

To serve
150g crème fraîche
a bunch of fresh chives, chopped

Melt the butter in a hot pan, add the shallot and
garlic, and cook until translucent. Add the artichokes,
thyme and bay leaves, and cook with the lid on until
soft, about 15 minutes.

Add the fish stock, and simmer until the artichokes
become very soft, another 5 minutes or so. Add the
double cream and the oysters and their liquor, and
bring to the boil. Liquidise and pass through a
chinois sieve into a clean pan.

Adjust the seasoning with salt and pepper. The soup
is now ready, served with a dollop of crème fraîche
and chopped chives.

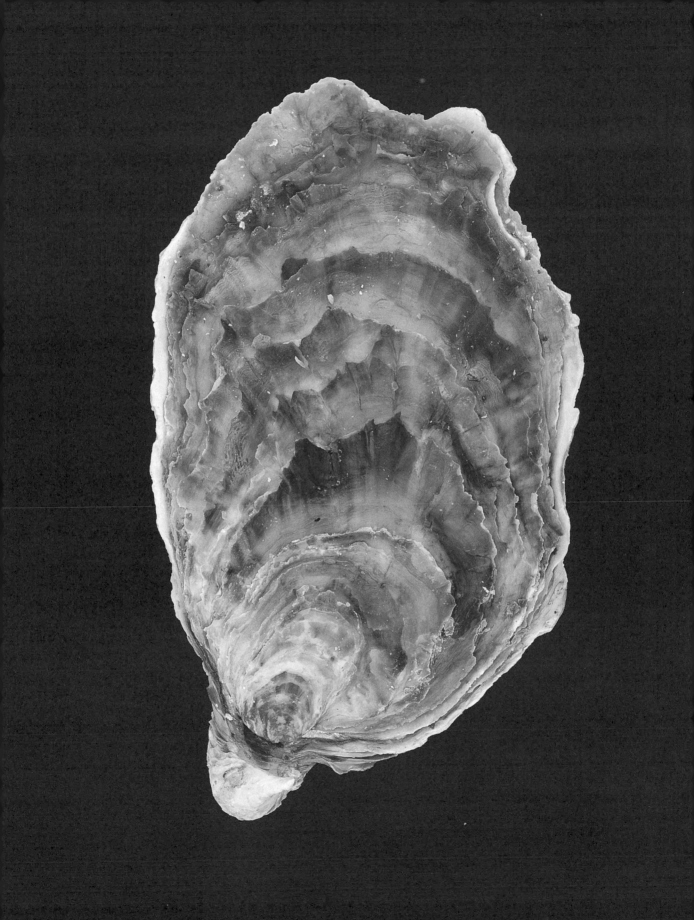

Sophie Grigson
Food writer

Smoked Haddock and Shrimp Chowder

Chowders are big, hearty soups, quick to make and a delight to eat. Essential items are potatoes, carrots, celery, bacon and milk, and from then on you can extemporise. Fish of some sort is usual in a chowder – it was, after all, originally a fisherman's on-board meal – but not absolutely critical (see below). Smoked haddock gives a particularly fine flavour, while a handful of shrimps or prawns lifts it a cut above the ordinary, Make a meal of this one, serving it in deep generous bowlfuls with warm bread.

Serves 4 as a main course, 6 as a starter

Base ingredients
1 onion, chopped
30g butter
4 rashers back bacon, cut into small strips

Aromatics
1 bay leaf
2 tbsp chopped fresh parsley

Main ingredients
2 large carrots, thickly sliced
2 celery stalks, thickly sliced
1 green pepper, seeded and cut into

postage-stamp squares
2 medium potatoes, peeled and cut into 1cm cubes
30g plain flour
250g skinned smoked haddock fillet
110g peeled, cooked shrimps or prawns

Liquids
600ml milk
150ml water

Dressing up
a handful of freshly grated Cheddar

Fry the onion and bacon gently in the butter until the onion is translucent and soft.

Now add the aromatics, using only half the parsley, and all the vegetable main ingredients. Stir around, then sprinkle over the flour, a little salt (not too much as both the bacon and the haddock may be salty) and plenty of pepper. Stir again for some 30 seconds or so to make sure the flour is more or less evenly distributed.

Now add a third of the milk and stir well, before adding the remaining milk, the water, and some more salt and pepper if needed. Bring up to the boil, stirring frequently to prevent catching. Turn the heat down low and simmer very gently for around 15-20

minutes until the vegetables are all tender. Stir frequently to prevent catching (i.e. burning) on the base. If the mixture seems too thick, add a little more milk or water.

While the soup simmers, cut the smoked haddock fillet into chunks about 2.5cm square, discarding any bones you may come across. Stir the haddock and the shrimps or prawns into the chowder and cook for a further 3-4 minutes until the haddock is just cooked through.

Serve in big bowlfuls, sprinkled with the remaining parsley and plenty of cheese.

(From *The First-time Cook*, Collins, 2004)

Spring

Early Rhubarb, Radishes, Parsley, Sardines, Sorrel, Beetroot, Mint, Spinach, Spring Lamb, Morel Mushrooms, Wild Garlic, Kale, Watercress, Sea Trout, Asparagus, Cherries, Cauliflower, Sea Bass, Raspberries, Broad Beans, Lemon Sole, New Carrots, Spring Greens, Wild Rocket, Leeks, Chives, Wild Fennel.

David Everitt-Matthias
Champignon Sauvage, Cheltenham, Gloucestershire

Nettle Velouté

Soups are one of the fun things to make in the kitchen, as they are only restricted by your imagination. The best soups are made only with the finest ingredients, don't just look at them as a way to use up leftovers, give them a little more respect. When handling nettles, at all stages of collection and preparation, use gloves. It is the heat of the boiling soup that kills the sting, making them safe to touch and eat.

Serves 6

100g white of leek, finely sliced
50g celery, chopped
120g onions, chopped
150g potato, peeled and diced
50g unsalted butter
600ml Vegetable Stock (see page 19)
250ml milk
100g fine pancetta slices
200g leek greens, finely sliced
500g young nettles
120ml double cream
salt and pepper to taste

Savoury Madeleines
50g ground almonds
50g plain flour
3 egg whites
85g butter, melted
a pinch of baking powder
100g leeks, washed and finely sliced
60g pancetta, finely diced

Preheat the oven to 180ºC/Gas 4.

To start the soup, sweat the leek white, celery, onion and potato for 5 minutes without colour in 25g of the butter. Pour on the stock and milk, bring to the boil, and simmer for 15 minutes.

Meanwhile, cook the pancetta slices in the preheated oven or grill until crisp. Leave to cool.

Start to make the Madeleines. Melt the butter until golden brown. Pass through a fine strainer, and cool. Fry the pancetta in a hot pan to release the fat, then add the leek and sweat until cooked. Cool.

Mix the ground almonds, flour, baking powder and egg whites. Gradually incorporate the melted butter, then mix in the diced pancetta and leek.

Place in a buttered Madeleine tray and bake in the preheated oven until golden brown and puffed up – about 10 minutes for small ones, 15 minutes for larger ones.

Meanwhile, to finish the soup, add the green of leek, simmer for 3 minutes more then add the nettles. Simmer for a few more minutes.

Liquidise, pass through a fine sieve, pushing hard to get all the purée through. Whisk in the double cream and remaining butter, and check the seasoning.

Crumble up the pancetta slices and sprinkle on the soup. Serve the Madeleines warm with the soup.

Galton Blackiston
Morston Hall, Morston, Norfolk

Asparagus Soup

I always look forward to those 6 weeks from the middle of May until the end of June with great excitement, heralding the arrival of Norfolk asparagus. I'm sure other counties will say the same, but I reckon Norfolk asparagus is the best, and this recipe is born from all the trimmings left when preparing asparagus the way we do at Morston Hall... And of course, being a proprietor, I hate wasting anything.

Serves 8–10

3 large bunches Norfolk asparagus
125g salted butter
1 large onion, thinly sliced
1 small potato, thinly sliced
1.2 litres Chicken or Vegetable Stock (see pages 21 or 19)
175g spinach leaves
150ml double cream
salt and pepper to taste

Cut the asparagus tips off so they are about the length of your middle finger. Lightly peel the bottom 2.5cm towards the cut end to create a neat white stalk and a plump green top. Retain the peelings. Chop the stalks and add to the peelings.

In a large pan, melt 55g of the butter over a medium heat, then add the sliced onion and potato. In another saucepan heat the stock. Once the onions and potatoes are soft, add the asparagus stalks and trimmings, and pour in the hot stock. Bring to the boil and simmer until the stalks are tender. Meanwhile, blanch the asparagus tips in boiling salted water for about 3 minutes, then drain and refresh in cold water. When ready to serve, fry briefly in 15g of the remaining butter.

Take the soup pot off the heat, add the spinach and whizz up in a liquidiser or food processor. Finally, push through a fine sieve: the easiest way to do this, I find, is with the back of a ladle.

Just before serving, bring the soup back up to temperature, add the remaining butter and the cream, and check the seasoning.

Serve topped with the blanched, buttered asparagus tips and, if you like, a thin strip of crispy streaky bacon.

Jeremy Lee
Blueprint Café, South Bank, London

Spinach and Fennel Soup

This is a delicious soup, hearty and pleasingly rich made from simmering spinach with fennel. These are two potent flavours that blend beautifully together, requiring the addition of nothing more than a little cream to finish. The soup has a beautiful fresh colour and flavour, though care must be taken to not keep the soup warm for too long as its colour will diminish and its flavour weaken. If being made in advance, then cool swiftly and refrigerate until needed. Indeed it can be the case that less is more, and a bowl of seemingly simple vegetables simmered together and then made smooth, to be served up with a loaf of good bread and some equally good butter is a delicious repast.

Serves 6

60g unsalted butter
2 small onions, finely chopped
2 small fennel bulbs, finely chopped
1 small potato, peeled and chopped
1.75 litres water
salt and pepper to taste
700g spinach
4-5 tbsp double cream

In a great heavy pot, melt the butter. Fry the onion then the fennel gently for half an hour or so until completely softened.

Wash the potato pieces in cold water until quite clear of starch. Add to the pot with the water, salt and pepper. Simmer thus until the potato is fully cooked.

Pick through the spinach, removing any excess stalk. Plunge the leaves into plenty of cold water then drain, repeating two or three times until all trace of sand is gone. Stir the spinach into the simmering pot, then remove from the heat.

Liquidise the soup in small quantities until very smooth. For a very smooth finish, push the soup through a fine sieve. If required, correct the consistency with water and then add the cream. Reheat and serve.

Ben O'Donoghue

The Atlantic Bar and Grill, Soho, London

Chicken and Watercress Soup

A very simple and tasty soup that only requires a few simple ingredients. The most important thing is to make sure that your stock is tastes as good as it possibly can.

Serves 4

Stock
1kg chicken wings
1 medium white onion, diced
1 celery stalk, diced
1 tsp black peppercorns
1 bay leaf

Soup
1 large potato, peeled and diced
shredded chicken meat (removed from the stock bones)

salt and pepper to taste
2 bunches watercress or 1 x 250g supermarket bag watercress, washed and tough stalks removed extra virgin olive oil

To make the stock, place the chicken wings in a pot, cover with water and bring to the boil, then drain and rinse with fresh water. This is to basically get rid of the excess fat. Then place the wings in a clean pot and cover with cold water again. Add the remaining stock ingredients and bring to the boil. Turn the stock down to a simmer and cook for about an hour. Be sure to remove any fat and scum that comes to the surface. Add a little extra water if the level falls below the bones.

The next thing is to pass the stock through a sieve into another clean pot. Bring to the boil and add the diced potato. Simmer this until the potato breaks down and thickens the soup. Use a spoon to break up the potato if need be.

While this is happening, pick the meat off the chicken wings, discarding the bones and skin, and add the

meat to the soup base. Season with salt and pepper to taste.

Then, just before serving, chop the watercress and add it to the soup. Bring to the boil and serve with lashings of good extra virgin olive oil.

Easy peasy!

Dave Miney

Oxo Tower, South Bank, London

Chilled New Season Garlic and Salt Cod Soup with Sea Urchin

We serve this soup in the Oxo on warm summer nights, and it is perfect as an *amuse-bouche*.

Serves 4

380g salt cod, soaked for a minimum of 36 hours
2 leeks, white only, washed
100g unsalted butter
2 new season garlic bulbs, cloves separated
1 large potato, peeled, washed and chopped
575ml Bourride Stock (see right)
250ml whipping cream
750ml milk, divided into three equal measures
a few drops of olive oil
2 lobes sea urchin

Bourride base stock
4 garlic cloves
60ml olive oil
240g chopped onion
1 leek, washed and roughly chopped
peel of 1 orange
30g tomato
600ml Fish Stock (see page 23)
2 parsley stalks
1 bay leaf
1 sprig fresh thyme

The first thing to do is soak the salt cod in water, for a minimum of 36 hours, changing the water several times.

Make the bourride base stock (you can substitute this with fish stock but the bourride will give the finished soup extra depth). Chop up the garlic cloves and cook gently in a pan with the olive oil, onion and leek. Add the orange peel and tomato, the stock and herbs. Bring to the boil and simmer for 10 minutes. Remove from heat, cover and stand at room temperature for a further 20 minutes. Strain.

For the soup, sweat the leeks in butter until soft with no colour. Meanwhile blanch the garlic cloves three times in one of the measures of milk (these changes of milk will soften the garlic flavour and remove the bitterness, meaning that you won't be tasting this soup for 3 hours afterwards!). After this process, the garlic will be easy to pop out of its skin,

so add the cloves to the leeks and continue to cook until all is completely soft.

In a separate pan, gently bring the drained salt cod up to the boil in the second measure of milk. Don't overcook: a couple of minutes at a low simmer is enough. Remove the fish from the milk and flake into the leeks and garlic, removing any skin and bones in the process.

Add the potato and bourride stock to the fish, and bring to the boil. Add the cream and the final third of milk, and cook until the potato is cooked. Blend in a processor, and while still hot, pass through a fine sieve. Cool and chill.

To serve, pour into a chilled bowl. Drizzle with olive oil and top with the sea urchin.

Andre Garrett

Orrery, Marylebone, London

Velouté of Wild Garlic with Sautéed Frogs' Legs

I love soup, especially in the colder months. I like to cook whatever ingredient I am using as fast as possible, with just enough stock to moisten to keep the natural flavour. This is one of my favourite recipes as it is a really earthy, rich soup, and paired with the garlicky frogs' legs, you can really get stuck in. It is also a perfect way to embrace the short wild garlic season (6-8 weeks in April and May), the frogs' legs a perfect complement.

Serves 4

12 large frogs' legs
olive oil

Soup
100g unsalted butter
500g Italian white onions, chopped
salt and pepper to taste
200ml Chicken or Vegetable Stock (see pages 21 or 19)
200ml double cream
50g wild garlic leaves, picked and washed

Garlic and parsley butter
100g unsalted butter
20g fresh parsley, finely chopped
10g garlic, puréed with a knife
a few drops of lemon juice

For the soup, melt the butter in a large pan and add the onions. Season and sweat slowly for about 20 minutes to extract all the flavours and natural sweetness. Add the stock and cook fast to reduce by half, then add the cream, bring back to the boil and simmer gently for 5 minutes.

Remove from the heat and add the garlic. Blitz the soup very well in a blender and pass through a fine sieve. Check the seasoning and put in a bowl over ice to cool quickly and keep the bright green colour.

For the garlic and parsley butter, simply mix all the ingredients in a bowl, season and set aside.

For the frogs' legs, detach the legs from the back-bone and clean back the shinbone on each leg for eating. Sauté the frogs' legs in a hot pan in a little oil. When they are coloured, add a few spoonfuls of garlic butter and finish cooking, but be careful not to burn the butter.

Reheat the soup once you have the frogs' legs ready in the butter. I like to serve this soup as a little amuse-gueule (pre-starter) to start the meal, the soup in one little cup and the frogs' legs and some butter in another little cup together.

Richard Corrigan
Lindsay House, Soho, London

Spring Vegetable Soup with Bacon Dumplings

Serves 6

1.5 litres Vegetable Stock (see page 19)
a small bunch of fresh thyme
olive oil
½ small onion, chopped
1½ garlic cloves, chopped
2 medium carrots, neatly chopped
1 celery stalk, neatly chopped
1 medium courgette, neatly chopped
1 small leek, washed and neatly chopped
salt and pepper to taste
freshly grated Parmesan, for serving

Dumplings
8 rashers good unsmoked bacon
olive oil
2 tbsp finely chopped onion
1 large garlic clove, chopped
2½ tbsp chopped fresh parsley
2½ tbsp chopped fresh tarragon

First make the dumplings. Cut the rinds off the bacon rashers: reserve the rinds for the soup. Mince the bacon very finely in a food processor. If the bacon is minced too coarsely it will not roll into dumplings and bind properly, and the dumplings will break up. Transfer the bacon to a bowl. Heat a film of oil in a frying pan, add the onion and garlic, and sweat over a low heat until soft but not coloured. Remove from the heat and stir in the parsley and tarragon. Leave to cool, then add to the minced bacon. Season to taste with pepper. Roll the mixture into walnut-sized dumplings, pressing firmly together. Keep, covered, in the fridge until ready to use.

For the soup, put the vegetable stock in a saucepan and add the bacon rinds and thyme. Bring to the boil and simmer for 15 minutes. Strain.

Heat a film of oil in the saucepan, add the onion and garlic and sauté over a moderate heat for about 2 minutes, stirring frequently. Add the carrots and sauté for 2 minutes. Add the celery and courgette, and sauté for another 2 minutes. Finally add the leek and sauté for 2 more minutes. Pour the stock into the pan and bring to the boil. Simmer for 7-8 minutes or until the vegetables are just tender but still a little crunchy.

Remove the pan from the heat and add the dumplings. Return to the heat and bring the soup almost to the boil. Simmer gently for 7 minutes.

Check the seasoning, then serve, sprinkled with Parmesan.

Jeff Baker

Pool Court at 42, Leeds, Yorkshire

Chilled Rhubarb 'Soup' with Poached Strawberries and Champagne Granita

I like the mixture of using luxury and 'peasant' produce to create this fine restaurant dish.

Serves 4

Granita
4 x 125ml glasses champagne (or cava)
125g caster sugar
juice and finely grated zest of 1 lemon

Soup
400g rhubarb
16 best strawberries
stock syrup (made by dissolving 125g caster sugar in 250ml water)

25ml Grenadine
250ml organic orange juice
1 vanilla pod, split
lemon balm leaves

Make the granita the day before. Put 1 glass of the champagne in a pan with the sugar, lemon zest and lemon juice. Heat to just below boiling point, then remove from the heat and leave to stand for 30 minutes to infuse. Add the remaining champagne after this time.

Place in a large bowl and leave to cool. Once cooled whisk vigorously, leave the whisk in the bowl and put in the freezer. Whisk vigorously again every 30 minutes until frozen and granular.

To make the 'soup', peel the rhubarb and cut into 16 batons, each 8cm long. Do not discard the trimmings. Wash and trim the strawberries.

Warm the stock syrup, Grenadine, orange juice and vanilla in a pan, add the rhubarb batons and trimmings, then poach until tender. Remove the batons and put on to a flat tray.

Next poach the strawberries in the poaching liquor, and remove with a slotted spoon once tender. Add the strawberries to the tray with the rhubarb and put the tray in the fridge to chill.

Liquidise the poaching liquor (including the rhubarb trimmings) then pass through a fine strainer or sieve. Leave to cool before chilling in the coldest part of the fridge overnight.

To serve, pre-chill the serving bowls. Place the rhubarb batons and strawberries in the bowls, then over these pour the chilled 'soup'.

Select the smallest leaves from the lemon balm to garnish with. Finally, spoon some of the granita into the centre of the soup, and serve immediately.

Chee Hwee Tong
Hakkasan, Fitzrovia, London

Lobster and Spinach Soup

This soup is delicious and has a wonderfully vibrant colour. Lightly blanched baby spinach, fresh enoki mushrooms and lobster tail combine to make this dish perhaps the most suave of broths. We chose to use lobster from the Caribbean as the meat has a really succulent texture and can be a little sweeter than its European counterparts. However, any good, fresh lobster will work just as well. Enjoy this soup straight from the wok. (Alan Yau)

Serves 4

600g baby spinach, washed
4 egg whites
160g Caribbean raw lobster tail (1 large or 2
small lobsters should provide enough meat)
vegetable oil, for frying
300g fresh enoki mushrooms, stalks removed
(buy in any good Chinese supermarket)
1 litre fresh stock (see page 16)
potato starch
salt to taste

Blanch the spinach in a pan of boiling water for 10 seconds or until just wilted. Drain off the water and squeeze the spinach lightly with tongs to expel any excess liquid. Place the spinach in a blender and blend on a high speed until very finely chopped. Whilst the blender is still running, but on a very low speed, slowly add the egg whites until the mixture becomes a thin paste/soup consistency. Leave to one side.

Prepare the lobster(s) by removing all parts of the shell where only the tail meat remains. Remove the skin from the tail meat and then slice into 12 equal-sized pieces (about 2-3cm each).

Heat the wok until smoking. Add 2 large ladles veg-etable oil, heat through until very hot and then add the lobster pieces, shallow-frying for approximately 1½ minutes. The lobster should only be half-cooked at this stage. Remove from the oil and leave to one side.

Clean out the wok, add 2 large ladles of water and bring to the boil. Blanch the mushrooms for 30 seconds. Remove the mushrooms from the wok and leave to one side.

Clean out the wok again, add the stock and warm through on a low heat for 2 minutes. Add the lobster pieces and leave to simmer in the stock for a further 1½ minutes. Next add the mushrooms and 6 pinch-es potato starch sprinkled in evenly. Stir gently. Finally, add the spinach paste. Stir gently and allow the whole soup to simmer for a further 30 seconds.

Turn out into 4 soup bowls, ensuring 3 pieces of lobster to each portion. Serve immediately without garnish.

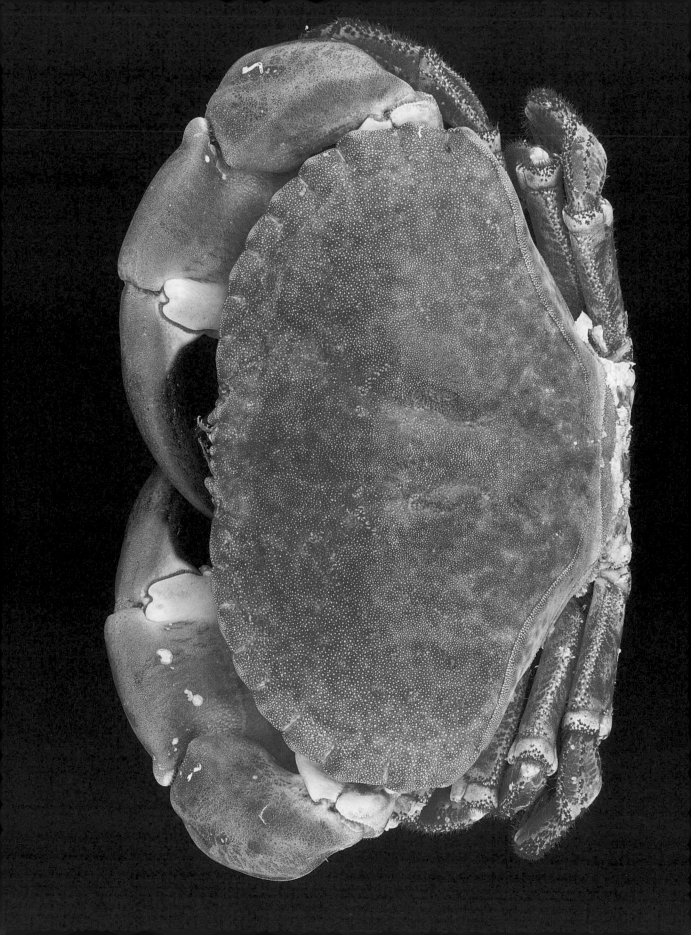

Mark Hix

J. Sheekey, Soho, London

Cornish Crab Soup

Serves 4-6

1kg freshly cooked whole crab
1 tbsp vegetable oil
1 small onion, roughly chopped
1 small leek, washed and roughly chopped
3 garlic cloves, roughly chopped
½ tsp fennel seeds
a few sprigs of fresh thyme
1 bay leaf
15g butter
1 tbsp tomato purée

1 tbsp plain flour
100ml white wine
1.5 litres Fish Stock (see page 23, but a cube will do)
100ml double cream

Remove the large claws and crack them carefully with a rolling pin or steak hammer. Remove the white meat with a teaspoon and put to one side, reserving the shells.

Hold the body shell with both hands and the smooth shell facing up. Push the shell up from the back with your thumbs to release it from the main body. Remove the grey gills (the dead man's fingers) that are attached to the body and discard. With a heavy chopping knife or meat cleaver, break the body and legs shells up into small pieces.

Heat a large heavy-bottomed saucepan with the vegetable oil and fry the crab shells on a high heat for about 5 minutes, stirring every so often until they begin to colour. Add the onion, leek, garlic, fennel seeds, thyme and bay leaf and continue cooking for another 5 minutes or so until the vegetables begin to colour.

Add the butter and stir well, then add the tomato purée and flour, stir well and cook for a minute or so

on a low heat. Add the white wine, then slowly add the fish stock, stirring to avoid any lumps.

Bring to the boil, season and simmer for 1 hour. Drain the soup, shells and all, in a colander over a bowl, stirring the shells so that any small pieces go into the liquid.

Remove about one-third of the crab shells (use the softer white body shells, as the claw and main shell are very hard) and put them in with the liquid and discard the rest. Liquidise the shells and liquid in a blender or food processor until smooth, then strain through a fine-meshed sieve.

Return to a clean pan, season with a little salt and pepper if necessary, and bring to the boil. To serve, add the cream and the crabmeat and stir well.

David Eyre

Eyre Brothers, Shoreditch, London

Portuguese Skate and Broad Bean Soup

Out of season you can use frozen baby broad beans or dried broad beans that have been soaked and cooked to al dente.

Serves 6-8

1 skate wing, around 400-500g, skinned
500g broad beans, podded
1 leek, washed
1 onion
1 carrot
1 green pepper, seeded
5 garlic cloves
1-2 fresh chillies, seeded
100ml olive oil
salt to taste

1 large waxy potato, peeled and cut into
5mm dice
2 litres Fish Stock (see page 23)

To serve
2-3 tbsp chopped fennel herb
4 spring onions, sliced
juice of 1 lemon

Remove the flesh from the skate wing, and cut into pieces that can be handled with a soup spoon.

Blanch the podded broad beans in boiling water until the skins can be popped off when pinched between thumb and forefinger. Don't skip this skinning – broad bean skins are nasty.

Chop finely the leek, onion, carrot, green pepper, garlic and chilli, and gently cook in a soup pot with the olive oil and a little salt, until all are soft and shiny.

Add the potato and stock to the pot. Bring to a slow simmer and cook until the potatoes are soft but not broken up. Add the skate pieces and the shelled broad beans and continue cooking at a simmer for a few minutes until the skate is just cooked.

Ladle into shallow bowls, and scatter some chopped fennel herb and some sliced spring onions into each bowl. Garnish further with a squeeze of lemon and some more olive oil. Eat with toasted cornbread or Portuguese broa.

Thomasina Miers
Winner, MasterChef

Tortilla Soup

This is a Mexican classic. It's simple, but at the same time sophisticated; it's easy to make yet creates a wow when you put it down on the table. You can make it with bits of leftover chicken for the perfect, comforting soup for hangovers or invalids, or you can make it as below for a lighter, more fragrant version. Either way you'll fall in love with it and make it again and again and again. I guarantee it!

Serves 4

1.2 litres chicken stock (see page 21)
1 onion, peeled and cut into 6 pieces
3 garlic cloves, peeled
1 x 400g can tomatoes or 4-6 fresh tomatoes,
skinned and seeded
6 corn tortillas
5 tbsp olive or vegetable oil
1-2 dried ancho chilli, stem and seeds removed
(see note below)
200g buffalo mozzarella or barrel-aged feta,
diced in ½ cm pieces

1 large, ripe avocado, diced as with the cheese
1 large lime, cut into wedges

Put the onion and garlic in a large, heavy frying pan on a fairly hot flame, and dry toast for 5-6 minutes until they start to take on a golden colour, stirring regularly. Put them in a food processor or blender with the tomatoes and whiz to a purée. Put the purée in a saucepan on a medium-high heat and reduce to a thick, tomato purée. Add the stock and simmer for 25 minutes. Season to taste, bearing in mind that feta is saltier than mozzarella. (This can be done the day before.)

Put the chilli in a dry frying pan and toast for 30 seconds – be careful not to burn it or the chilli will taste bitter. Tear into strips.

Cut the tortillas in half and then cut each half into 2 cm long strips. Heat the oil in a saucepan until shimmering (test with a tortilla strip to see if it sizzles which means the oil is hot enough). Add half the strips and fry, stirring constantly until the pieces are golden brown and crispy. Take out and dry on kitchen paper. Repeat with the remaining strips; you can re-use the oil for another recipe.

When you are ready to eat divide the tortilla strips and chilli strips between 4 bowls. Add the tomato broth. On the table arrange the cheese, avocado and lime wedges so that each person can add liberally to their soup, squeezing on the lime juice. You may also like to chop some flat leaf parsley or coriander to garnish (the Mexicans use a herb called epazote if you can find it).

Note
Several companies now supply Mexican chillies in this country, but if you can't get hold of ancho chillies, add a little smoked paprika to your broth and a little fresh chilli or even some strips of sun-dried tomato for a slightly different twist.

Fergus Henderson
St John, Clerkenwell, London

New Season Garlic and Bread Soup

This is a very simple, but reviving and steadying soup. For the early months of spring you can get fresh garlic before it is dried. It has a longer, greener stem, giving you the flavour of garlic with a youthful nature. A mouli is very useful for this recipe – in fact a mouli is useful all the time.

Serves 6

8 fresh whole garlic bulbs
1 litre Chicken Stock (see page 21)
salt and pepper to taste
a healthy handful of chunks, without crust,
of yesterday's – if not even the day before's –
white bread

Place the garlic in the stock and bring to the boil, then reduce to a simmer until the garlic is cooked soft, approximately 40 minutes. Then pass the garlic through the mouli (if you have no mouli, press it through a sieve).

Mix the garlic pulp back into the stock and season to taste. Reheat and throw in the bread a couple of minutes before serving, so it has just long enough to sup up the soup but not fall apart.

Marco Pierre White
Mirabelle, Mayfair, London

Truffled Parsley Soup with Poached Egg

This soup can be served and enjoyed all year round. Truffle oil is slightly less expensive than truffles themselves, but still adds its unique flavour.

Serves 4

50g fresh parsley
200g fresh spinach leaves, washed
1 litre Chicken Stock (see page 21)
150g smoked bacon, sliced
750ml double cream
salt and pepper to taste
truffle oil
1 tsp white wine vinegar
4 eggs
12 sprigs fresh flat-leaf parsley

Bring a large pan of salted water to the boil. Add the 50g parsley and after 3 minutes the spinach, and cook for another 3 minutes until tender. Drain, and blend to a purée in a liquidiser. Pass the purée through a fine sieve, and chill in the fridge. Put the chicken stock and smoked bacon into a pan and reduce by three-quarters (to 250ml). Then add the double cream and reduce further. Sieve to remove the bacon.

Bring the cream mixture back to the boil, and add 1 tbsp of the truffle oil and the parsley purée. The colour should be rich green.

Bring a small pan of water to the boil, add the white wine vinegar, and bring the temperature up to 100ºC. Turn down the flame, and break the eggs into the pan. After a few minutes remove them and refresh in iced water to stop them cooking further. Trim the egg whites neatly with a knife, and reheat in hot salted water just before serving.

Place a poached egg in each soup bowl, pour the soup over, and garnish each with 3 sprigs of flat-leaf parsley and a little truffle oil.

(From *The Mirabelle Cookbook*, Ebury Press, 1999)

Mitchell Tonks
Founder of Fishworks

Fish Stew with Langoustines

I first made this fish stew whilst sailing with my young son in the Greek islands. We moored up with our bag of fish that we had bought earlier, and a handful of basic ingredients, sat on the beach and cooked the fish using seawater as our stock. It was fantastic, and not only that, the shoreline was littered with sea urchins, and the pair of us sat there, cracking them open, and enjoying every single one. It still rates as one of the best meals I've ever eaten. With the luxury of a few langoustines added, this easy soup is real winner.

Serves 4

1 shallot, finely chopped
2 garlic cloves, chopped
olive oil
2 tomatoes, roasted
a pinch of saffron strands
3-4 sprigs fresh thyme
a splash of Pernod
200ml white wine

selection of fish (lobster, clams, mussels, chunks of skate, steaks of hake, gurnard and cod), about 400g, enough to fill the pan packed tightly in one layer
6 langoustines
sea salt to taste

Aïoli
2 egg yolks
1 tsp Dijon mustard
4 garlic cloves, crushed to a paste
150ml good olive oil
juice of ½ lemon

To serve
chopped fresh parsley
grilled bread

To make the aïoli, put the egg yolks in a bowl with the mustard and garlic. Whilst whisking add the olive oil in a steady stream until a thick emulsion is formed. Add the lemon juice, season with a little sea salt, and let it stand for an hour before serving.

To make the soup, in a large pan sweat the shallot and garlic together in a little olive oil. Add the tomatoes, saffron and thyme and stir together. Add the Pernod and tip the pan away from you allowing it to catch fire and burn off the alcohol. Add the wine and simmer gently for 2 minutes. Add the fish with enough water to just cover it, and simmer for 8-10 minutes.

Remove the thyme and season with some sea salt. Finally sprinkle with fresh chopped herbs and accompany with grilled bread topped with rich, garlicky aïoli.

Summer

Grey mullet, Gooseberries, Tayberries,
Courgettes, Broad Beans, Welsh Lamb,
Elderflowers, Lettuce, Crab, Strawberries,
Peppers, Asparagus, Redcurrants, Salmon,
Cherries, Peas, Blueberries, Clams, Aubergines,
Fennel, Tomatoes, Trout, Watercress, Basil,
Loganberries, Sage, Raspberries, Broccoli,
Greengages, Hare, Skate, John Dory

Herbert Berger
1 Lombard Street, City, London

Chilled Cucumber Soup with Oriental Spices

This is great for summer and, if you like, you can add fresh shellfish like crab, lobster, prawns and so on.

Serves 4-6

Part 1
**1 large cucumber, peeled and chopped but
not seeded
2 garlic cloves
½ stick lemongrass
10g pickled sushi ginger
1 lime leaf
1 small sprig fresh mint
1 small sprig fresh Thai basil
1 small bunch fresh coriander
1 small fresh chilli**

**juice of 1 lime
a pinch of ground cumin
salt and pepper to taste**

Part 2
**250ml coconut milk
500ml organic live yoghurt
sesame oil
fresh Thai basil leaves**

Place all the ingredients from part 1 in a bowl, and marinate in the fridge for 4-6 hours.

Put in a food processor together with the coconut milk and most of the yoghurt, and blend until fine. Adjust the seasoning and pass through a coarse sieve.

Serve in chilled bowls and garnish with some yoghurt, sesame oil and Thai basil leaves.

Mark Broadbent

Bluebird Dining Room, Chelsea, London

Iced Cornish Crab Gazpacho Andaluz

The inspiration for this dish came from my favourite little coastal village, Cadaques in Catalunya.

Serves 6

1 large cock crab, cooked
20 over-ripe vine tomatoes, roughly chopped
2 cucumbers, peeled, seeded and chopped
20 piquillo wood-roast peppers, chopped
8 garlic cloves, minced
1 ciabatta loaf (stale), crust removed, cut into small chunks
300ml tomato passata or rich tomato juice
1 red chilli, seeded and finely chopped
300ml Extra virgin Arbequina olive oil

1 generous tbsp sherry vinegar Jerez-Valdespino
still mineral water as necessary
salt and pepper to taste

To serve
tiny croûtons
cucumber, peeled and diced
extra virgin olive oil
flat-leaf parsley, chopped

Marinate all the ingredients - except for the crab, water and seasoning - together for 12 hours.

Take the large cock crab, and crack open. Separate the brown meat and juices and the white meat, and check both thoroughly for any bits of shell.

Blend the gazpacho mix in a blender, adding the brown crab and juices, and adding still mineral water for consistency. Check the seasoning and pass through a conical strainer.

Serve with a little crushed ice, croûtons, cucumber dice, the fresh white crab, a drizzle of olive oil and some parsley.

Gary Rhodes

Rhodes Twenty Four, City, London

Pea Soup

Serves 4 (as a generous starter)

600ml water (stock could also be used, see pages 14-23)
450g podded peas (frozen can also be used)
salt and pepper to taste
a pinch of caster sugar
100ml whipping or single cream

Bring the water or stock to the boil in a saucepan and add the peas. Bring back to the boil and cook for 5 minutes until tender (longer if necessary). Remove from the heat, season with salt, pepper and a pinch of sugar, and liquidise to a smooth creamy soup.

For the smoothest of finishes, strain through a sieve. The soup at this stage can be cooled over ice to help maintain its colour then simply re-heated when needed.

If serving immediately, add the cream and return to a gentle simmer, seasoning once again with salt and pepper.

Note
For an added twist to this soup and to transform it into a tasty main course, ladle the soup around a pan-fried fillet of fresh cod topped with toasted sesame seeds and finished with a drop or two of sesame oil.

A little chopped mint can be added to the soup, creating the classic pea and mint combination.

A sprinkling of flavoured stock cube (chicken or vegetable) can be added to the water, offering a slightly stronger finish to the soup.

Eric Treuille
Books for Cooks, Notting Hill, London

Corn Soup with Red Pepper Purée

A stunning soup, both colour and flavour wise. The pepper purée makes a pretty red centre in this pale yellow soup, and its smokey heat perfectly complements the natural sweetness of the corn.

Serves 4

30g butter
1 onion, chopped
2 garlic cloves, chopped
1 carrot, chopped
1 leek, white parts only, chopped
1 litre hot stock (see pages 14-23) or water
6 corn cobs, kernels stripped with a sharp knife (or use 500g frozen sweetcorn kernels)
salt and pepper to taste
1 tbsp lemon juice
4 tbsp double cream

Red pepper purée
2 red peppers, quartered and seeded
1 small garlic clove, crushed
Tabasco sauce

For the purée, put the pepper quarters under a hot grill until charred and blistered all over. Put the peppers in a bowl, cover with a plate, and leave for 10 minutes while the trapped steam loosens the skins so they may easily be slipped off. Put the peeled peppers into a blender or food processor with the garlic and a few tbsp of the stock for the soup and pulse to a purée. Push through a sieve for absolute smoothness and add salt, pepper and Tabasco to taste.

Melt the butter in a heavy pot, add the onion, garlic, carrot and leek and cook gently over a low heat, stirring occasionally, until soft and wilted, about 15 minutes. Pour in the hot stock or water, raise the heat and simmer gently until the vegetables are done, about 10 minutes – you should easily be able to crush a piece of carrot with a wooden spoon against the side of the pan.

Add the corn, raise the heat, and, as soon as the soup is at a rolling boil, turn off the heat at once. Cover and leave for about 3 minutes before puréeing the soup very thoroughly in a blender or food processor – leave it whizzing for at least 3 minutes.

Return the soup to the rinsed-out pan, thin with water if necessary and add salt and pepper to taste. Stir in the lemon juice and cream and reheat until piping hot but not boiling.

Ladle the hot soup into warmed bowls and drop a spoonful of the red pepper purée into the middle of each soup. Serve at once.

(From *One Year at Books for Cooks*, No. 3, Pryor Publications, 1997)

Nino Sassu
Assaggi, The Chepstow, Bayswater, London

Clam and Fregola Soup

This is a typical Sardinian soup made with clams and fregola, a type of coarse couscous. The soup should be of medium thickness, not too liquid and not too dry, and should be served with a nice dry white wine. It is quite easy to make, and the ingredients listed below should be sufficient for two or three, depending how greedy you are with the portions.

Serves 2-3

600g clams
100ml dry white wine
2 tbsp extra virgin olive oil
1 garlic clove, finely chopped
1 small bunch fresh parsley, finely chopped
1 fresh chilli, seeded and finely chopped
2 ripe vine tomatoes, skinned and chopped
100g fregola (or coarse couscous)
salt and pepper to taste
6 basil leaves

Rinse and wash the clams thoroughly in cold water twice, and then soak in clean fresh water for about 3 hours.

After the 3 hours, drain and place the clams in a large saucepan over heat. Stir to allow the clams to open. Once opened, add the white wine and let it evaporate for a minute or so. When cool enough to handle, separate the shells from the clam meat, and discard the shells. Drain the liquid through a fine sieve or a piece of muslin, and reserve with the clams.

In a separate saucepan heat the olive oil, and fry the finely chopped garlic, parsley and chilli for a few minutes on a medium heat. Add the chopped tomatoes, then stir to amalgamate all the ingredients and cook for about 5 minutes. Add the fregola and let it absorb the flavours of the sauce for a minute or so.

Add the liquid from the clams and about 750ml water and cook for a further 10-12 minutes or until the fregola is cooked to your liking. Add the clams and salt to taste. Tear the basil leaves and add them to the soup. Serve hot.

Adam Byatt

Thyme, The Hospital, Covent Garden, London

Soup of Roast Chicken, Peas and Sweetcorn

This soup is a simple combination of familiar flavours, technical in preparation, simple in presentation, yet delicious. The roast chicken jelly is savoury, the peas have their own unique sweetness, and the sweetcorn is delicate and delicious. The tarragon helps to bring all three together.

Serves 10

Chicken jelly
1kg chicken wings
1 carrot, 1 leek and 1 celery stalk, trimmed and cut into tiny dice (mirepoix)
1 sprig fresh thyme
2 garlic cloves
2 sprigs fresh tarragon

Pea mousse
1kg fresh podded peas
1 onion, diced
100g butter
600ml double cream
4 gelatine leaves

Sweetcorn velouté
1 onion, diced
100g butter
1 garlic clove
1 sprig fresh thyme
500ml double cream
800ml milk
800ml water
1 x 500g can quality sweetcorn

Garnish
1 tray fresh pea shoots

Preheat the oven to 200ºC/Gas 6.

For the chicken jelly, chop the chicken wings. Roast in the preheated oven until thoroughly caramelised, up to about an hour. Add the mirepoix vegetables, thyme and garlic. Cover with water and cook gently for 3 hours. Sieve the stock, then infuse with fresh tarragon, and place in a bowl in the fridge to chill. In advance of serving, heat up and place about 150ml in the bottom of individual serving bowls. Chill to set.

To make the pea mousse, sweat the onion in the butter, then add 500ml of the cream, and bring to the boil. Add the shelled peas. Once the peas are cooked, blend the contents and pass through a fine sieve. Soak the gelatine leaves in water, then drain and add to the purée. Leave the purée in the fridge,

where it will set firm. Once set, add the remaining 100ml of cream, lightly whipped. Pass through a fine sieve to achieve a mousse-like texture.

To make the sweetcorn velouté, sweat the onion in the butter with the garlic and thyme until soft; then add the cream, milk and water. Bring to the boil and add the sweetcorn. Boil gently for 30 minutes until cooked, then blend to a velvety textured soup.

To serve, have ready the bowls with the set chicken jelly in them. Warm the sweetcorn velouté, foam with a hand blender, then pour the foam over the jelly. Place a small quenelle of pea mousse over the velouté. Garnish the bowl with fresh pea shoots and serve immediately.

Alfred Prasad

Tamarind, Mayfair, London

Tomato Rasam

A stimulating thin soup of tomatoes flavoured with coriander, garlic and peppercorns.

Serves 4

4 ripe tomatoes
4 tsp split yellow lentils (toor dal)
½ bunch fresh coriander
4 garlic cloves
6 black peppercorns
¼ tsp cumin seeds
¼ tsp red chilli powder
1 pinch turmeric powder
salt to taste

1 tbsp vegetable oil
¼ tsp mustard seeds
2 sprigs curry leaves
¼ tsp ground asafoetida

To temper
Wash and chop the tomatoes and keep aside. Wash the lentils and boil until soft in 1.2 litres water. Strain and keep both the lentils and liquid aside. Wash the coriander, chop the leaves and keep the stalks as well. Crush the garlic (with skin), and grind roughly with the peppercorns and cumin seeds. Leave to one side.

Put the strained lentil water to boil along with the tomatoes, roughly ground garlic, peppercorns and cumin and the coriander stalks. Add the chilli and turmeric, and leave to simmer for 15 minutes or until the tomatoes are mashed. Strain the soup and add the chopped coriander leaves.

For the tempering, heat the oil in a pan, add the mustard seeds and as they begin to crackle, throw in the curry leaves and asafoetida. Add the tempering to the strained soup, and mix well. Bring to the boil, add salt to taste, and serve hot.

Ian Wood

Almeida, Islington, London

Chilled Vine Tomato and Olive Oil Soup

Serves 4

1.2 kg vine tomatoes (over-ripe are better)
1 garlic clove
15g salt
5g freshly ground white pepper
50ml olive oil
50ml red wine vinegar
500ml tomato passata
1 small bunch fresh basil

Boil a kettle full of water and pour over the tomatoes. Wait for 20-30 seconds. Core and peel the tomatoes, and place in a container large enough to hold all the ingredients.

Peel and crush the garlic and add to the tomatoes. Add the rest of the ingredients and leave to marinate for at least 24 hours.

Blitz in a processor or blender, and pass through a fine sieve or chinois.

Serve chilled with a garnish of white crab meat or tapenade croûtons.

Prue Leith

Hoxton Apprentice, Hoxton, London

Tomato and Basil Soup

This is a glorious fresh-tasting soup. Preparing the tomatoes takes a bit of time but is definitely worth it.

Serves 6

2.3 kg tomatoes
24 large fresh basil leaves
170g salted butter
salt and pepper to taste
85g fromage blanc

Make a small slit in the skin of each tomato and blanch in boiling water for 5-7 seconds. They are ready to peel when the skin starts to lift away from the knife slits. Skin, then halve the tomatoes, scooping the seeds and juice into a sieve set over a bowl. Sieve the juice and reserve, then cut the tomato flesh into small strips.

Roughly chop all but 6 of the basil leaves. Put the tomato strips, reserved juice and chopped basil into a large deep frying pan. Add 55g of the butter and place over a medium heat, shaking the pan and stirring.

When the tomato strips start to break up, turn up the heat and briskly stir in the remaining butter. When all the butter has been added, the tomatoes should be only half cooked. Season to taste with salt and pepper.

Fill individual soup bowls with the tomato soup, then spoon fromage blanc into the middle of each bowl. Garnish each soup with a fresh basil leaf and serve immediately.

Mark Hix

The Ivy, Covent Garden, London

Iced Plum Tomato Soup with Basil and Mozzarella

This eternally popular soup wasn't originally made for the restaurant at all: it was a staple of the outside catering business. We must have served it a thousand times before it finally got put on the menu. It was an immediate success. It is a simple dish to make but do not be tempted to use anything other than ripe plum tomatoes or other well-flavoured ones. It is an intensely flavoured soup and therefore served in small quantities.

Serves 4-6

500g soft plum tomatoes, halved and seeded
500g cherry tomatoes
300ml tomato juice
3 tsp balsamic vinegar
1 garlic clove, blanched in water for 2 minutes
salt and pepper to taste

Garnish
150g mozzarella cheese
(baby ones if possible), sliced

60ml basil and olive oil purée (simply blitz together), or pesto
a handful of small basil leaves (purple if possible)
150g mixed tomatoes, cherry, yellow, plum etc., cut into small pieces

Process the plum tomatoes in a blender with the cherry tomatoes, tomato juice, balsamic vinegar and garlic, and pass the mixture through a fine sieve. Correct the seasoning to taste, adding a little more balsamic vinegar if necessary.

Chill the soup in the freezer for 20-30 minutes. Serve in a soup plate with small slices of mozzarella, basil purée, small basil leaves, and a selection of tomato pieces.

Raymond Blanc

Le Manoir aux Quat' Saisons, Great Milton, Oxfordshire

Maman Blanc's Vegetable and Chervil Soup

A small tribute to Maman Blanc. And I should say to Papa Blanc, too, as most of the vegetables would come from his garden. The success of this soup depends upon the freshness and quality of the vegetables used. However, you can vary the vegetables and herbs according to the season. Chervil is one of my favourite herbs and is very popular in France but less well known in the UK, although you can now find it in most supermarkets.

Serves 4-6

1 onion, cut into 3mm dice
1 garlic clove, crushed
2 large carrots, cut into slices 3mm thick
3 celery stalks, cut into slices 5mm thick
2 leeks, washed and outer layers removed,
cut into slices 1cm thick
15g unsalted butter
salt and white pepper to taste
1 large courgette, halved lengthways and cut
into slices 5mm thick
2 ripe tomatoes, roughly chopped

1 litre boiling water
1 large handful fresh chervil, roughly chopped

To serve
1 tbsp crème fraîche or 15g unsalted butter

Over a medium heat, in a large saucepan, soften the onion, garlic, carrots, celery and leeks in the butter for 5 minutes, without letting them colour (this helps to extract maximum flavour). Season with 8 pinches of salt and 2 pinches of white pepper.

Add the courgette, tomato and boiling water (using boiling water reduces the cooking time and also helps keep the colours bright). Boil fast for 5-7 minutes, until the vegetables are just tender. Stir in the chopped chervil.

Whisk in the crème fraîche or butter (or both, if you wish). Taste and correct the seasoning if necessary, then serve. This soup can be puréed in a blender if you prefer a smooth texture.

Michael Caines
Gidleigh Park, Chagford, Devon

Vegetable and Herb Soup

This is a simple and wonderful soup for the summer, full of flavour yet light and fresh. If you are vegetarian then simply replace the chicken stock with water. The vegetable dice don't have to be exactly 10mm, but make sure they are the same size so that you get even cooking through the vegetables. You can use different types of herbs to introduce different flavours, which will enhance the soup, but make sure they are fresh and added at the last moment so their colour and flavour are retained.

Serves 4-5

20g finely chopped shallot
35g finely diced leek
50g finely diced celeriac
50g finely diced carrot
150g unsalted butter
salt and pepper to taste
50ml white wine
500ml water
500ml Chicken Stock (optional, see page 21)
50g finely diced courgette

50g French beans
50g podded peas
50g finely diced cabbage
100ml double cream
12 fresh basil leaves, roughly chopped
5g each of fresh sorrel, chervil and chives, chopped
50g blanched, seeded and finely diced tomato
a pinch of caster sugar

Sweat the shallot, leek, celeriac and carrot in 25g of the butter with a pinch of salt for 5 minutes without colouring. Add the white wine and reduce to virtually nothing, then add the water and chicken stock and bring to the boil, and cook for about 10 minutes.

Add the courgette, French beans, peas and cabbage and cook for a further 5 minutes.

Now add the cream and whisk in the remaining butter. Add the herbs and tomato, and season with salt, pepper and a pinch of sugar.

Enjoy!

Richard Guest

The Castle Hotel, Taunton, Somerset

Cauliflower Cheese Soup

A bowl of soup is something we all understand, we know why we want to eat it and we know the brands and the flavours we prefer. So in my mind a soup should taste exactly of what it says it will, so what you've been yearning for all day isn't crushed in an instant or more probably an 'instant' soup.

Serves 4

1 small cauliflower
1 large potato
2 garlic cloves
850ml semi-skimmed milk
25g butter
2 tbsp freshly grated Parmesan
salt and white pepper to taste

Trim and finely chop the cauliflower. Peel and finely chop the potato. Peel and finely chop the garlic.

Put the cauliflower, potato, garlic and milk into a saucepan, and simmer on a low heat until the potato is very soft. Add the butter and Parmesan, and blend in a food processor until smooth. Pass through a fine sieve, and season to taste.

Reheat and serve.

Tom Aikens

Tom Aikens, Chelsea, London

Sweetcorn and Smoked Bacon Soup

Serves 4-6

50g unsalted butter
500g fresh sweetcorn kernels, cut from the cob
80g smoked streaky bacon, chopped
15g caster sugar
4g sea salt
4g fresh thyme
1.2 litres Chicken Stock (see page 21)
150ml double cream

Warm a pan on a low heat and melt the butter. Add the sweetcorn kernels, bacon, sugar, salt and thyme and cook slowly on a low heat with a lid on the pan for 5 minutes. Stir now and again so the mix does not colour but sweats in the steam.

Add the stock and cream, then turn the heat up, bring to a slow boil and simmer for 5 minutes. Remove from the heat and discard the thyme. Blend the soup to a fine purée.

Reheat and serve.

Gordon Ramsay
Restaurateur, food writer

Aubergine and Pepper Soup with Sautéed Cherry Tomatoes

Serves 4-6

4 medium aubergines
leaves from 1 sprig fresh rosemary
1 tbsp chopped garlic
olive oil, for frying
salt and pepper to taste
2 large red peppers
2 large yellow peppers
1 shallot, chopped

2 sprigs fresh basil
1 tbsp coarse-grain mustard
300ml Vegetable or Chicken Stock (see pages 19 and 21)
250ml tomato juice
200g cherry tomatoes on the vine

Preheat the oven to 190ºC/Gas 5.

Peel the skin from the aubergines in long strips using a swivel vegetable peeler, taking about 5mm of the flesh still attached to the skin. Cut the skin into long strips and then into small dice. Set aside.

Wrap the peeled aubergines in foil with the rosemary leaves and garlic. Roast for about 45 minutes or until the flesh has completely broken and softened. Save the cooking juices.

Heat about 2 tbsp olive oil in a large frying pan and, when hot, cook the soft aubergine flesh over a high heat to give it a slightly scorched flavour. Mix in the saved roasting juices and season. Remove from the pan and set aside to cool.

Stand the peppers upright on the board and cut the flesh from the central seed core and stalk. Chop the pepper flesh.

Add another tbsp or two of oil to the frying pan and, when hot, sauté the shallot until lightly coloured. Mix in the peppers and continue frying over a high

heat for about 5 minutes. Mix in the basil and mustard, and then the stock. Bring to the boil and season, then simmer for 12-15 minutes. Remove from the heat and cool.

Discard the basil, then pour the pepper mixture into a food processor or blender. Add the aubergine and whizz until creamy and smooth. The soup will be quite thick. Gradually mix in the tomato juice. Chill until ready to serve.

To prepare the garnish, heat a little oil in the frying pan and fry the reserved chopped aubergine until light and crisp. Drain on kitchen paper.

Pull the tomatoes from the stalks and fry them in a little more oil to flavour the skin. They will go a bit squashy, which is fine. Drain on kitchen paper.

Check the seasoning of the soup then pour into 4-6 chilled serving bowls. Divide the sautéed tomatoes among the bowls and scatter over the aubergine flakes.

From *A Chef for All Seasons*, Gordon Ramsay, Quadrille, 2000

Sally Clarke

Clarke's, Kensington, London

Soup of Five Tomatoes and Three Beetroots

This chilled soup was first placed on a dinner menu in a blisteringly hot summer a few years ago and because of its freshness and acidity, it became an instant success.

Serves 6

90ml olive oil
½ head new season garlic, roughly chopped
1 large onion, roughly chopped
4 celery stalks, roughly chopped
1 fennel bulb, roughly chopped
500g very ripe plum tomatoes, roughly chopped
500g very ripe beefsteak tomatoes, roughly chopped
250g medium to large red beetroot, cooked, peeled and roughly chopped

2 tbsp chopped fresh basil, plus the stalks
salt and pepper to taste

Garnish
50g two types of baby beetroot (any colour or shape – red, yellow, pink, round, long)
6 sprigs fresh basil
1 tbsp long cut chives, 2cm long
good olive oil
120g three types of tomatoes (any colour or shape – cherry red, cherry yellow, tear shaped)
120ml crème fraîche (optional)

Preheat the oven to 200ºC/Gas 6. In a heavy-based pan, gently heat the olive oil with the garlic, onion, celery and fennel, and cook them until they start to soften without browning. Add the tomatoes, beetroot, basil stalks, salt and pepper. Barely cover with water, bring to the boil, then place, uncovered, in the preheated oven for 40 minutes, or until all the vegetables are tender.

Liquidise, adding a little water if necessary, and pass through a sieve, pushing the debris with the underside of a ladle until almost dry. Taste for seasoning, check the consistency and chill in the refrigerator.

Cook the garnish beetroot in two separate pans of boiling salted water until tender, approximately 20-25 minutes. Drain, cool and peel under running cold water. Trim the tails and tops of the beetroot and cut into halves or quarters, depending on their size. If using different-coloured beetroot, keep the yellow

and red in separate bowls so that the colours do not stain. Season each bowl with a quarter of the basil leaves and chives, salt, pepper and a drizzle of olive oil.

Cut each type of garnish tomato, depending on its shape and size: some may need to be quartered whilst others may be small enough to keep whole. Place together in a bowl and season as before with the chives, and some of the remaining basil.

If at home, place 6 soup plates or bowls in the freezer at least an hour before serving. If out on a picnic, try to store the soup plates in a cool bag until required.

To serve, stir the soup well, check the seasoning and half fill each bowl. Spoon the garnish tomatoes and beetroots into the centre of each dish. Garnish with the remaining basil sprigs, a drizzle of good olive oil and a generous scoop of crème fraîche, if using.

(From *Sally Clarke's Book*, Grub Street, 2004)

Annabel Buckingham
Compiler, Soup Kitchen

Fat's Courgette Soup

This recipe was one of the fruits of a recent trip to the south coast to see my friends, the Sopers. Jon Soper - a former band member of Fat and Frantic (early 90s popsters in Madness/Housemartins' tradition) now leads a church in Exeter. As well as a reference to his band, Jon was also called 'Fat' at school because although not physically large, he could be relied on to be in a consistently 'fat' state of mind (i.e. supremely relaxed), a quality which remains with him to this day. During my stay, Jon made this courgette soup - his mum's creation – for us for supper. It's quick, easy, delicious and (in keeping with a theme) not altogether kind to the waistline.

Serves about 3-4, depending on hunger

450g courgettes
450ml Chicken Stock (see page 21)
225g full-fat cream cheese
1 tsp curry powder

Wash, top and tail the courgettes. Chop them into thick chunks and boil them in the chicken stock for 5 minutes.

Blend the mixture in a blender, and then stir in the cheese and curry powder. Serve immediately

Atul Kochar

Benares, Mayfair, London

Cold Soup of Yoghurt and Cucumber/ Dahi aur Kheerae ka Shorba

This is a beautiful soup for the hot days of an Indian summer. It is very like the chilled yoghurt drink from India – lassi – but it's not a sin to be a creative user of an idea.

Serves 4

1 green snubnose chilli
400g cucumber
200g natural yoghurt
1 tsp salt
10g toasted cumin seeds
4 sprigs fresh mint leaves

Slit the green chilli lengthways, remove the seeds and chop the flesh roughly. Peel the cucumber, remove the seeds with a sharp knife and cut the flesh into small pieces.

Liquidise the cucumber in small batches with the yoghurt and green chilli. Add the salt and toasted cumin while blending.

Keep the soup in the fridge to chill. Serve cold garnished with mint leaves.

Note
A snubnose chilli is a tiny, extremely pungent and spicy chilli.

Brian Turner

Brian Turner Mayfair, London

Green Pea and Ham Soup

There are so many versions of pea soup that to say one is the definitive classic recipe is practically impossible. Soup made from tinned peas is my least favourite but, if made from dried, fresh or a mixture, can work well. The following, however, is the one I like best.

Serves 8

75g butter
1 small onion, finely diced
900g frozen peas
1 sprig fresh mint
75g plain flour
275ml double cream
salt and pepper to taste

Ham stock
1 ham hock, about 900g in weight
3.6 litres water
2 carrots
2 onions
1 head celery, washed
12 black peppercorns
1 bay leaf

To start the stock, soak the ham hock for 12 hours in enough cold water to cover. Drain off the soaking water, then cover the ham hock with the measured cold water, bring to the boil and skim off any scum. Add the peeled carrots and onions and the celery. Leave to simmer gently for about 20 minutes, then add the peppercorns and bay leaf. Simmer for a further 2-2½ hours until the ham is cooked through. Strain off the stock for the soup – you will need 1.8 litres. Put the ham to one side, and discard the vegetables and flavourings.

Meanwhile, melt the butter in a heavy-bottomed pan, and add the finely diced onion and half the frozen peas. Add the mint, cover the pan and gently stew for 3-5 minutes. At this point add the flour and stir in carefully, possibly taking the pan off the heat to stop the sticking. Put the pan back on the heat and cook the pea roux for 2 minutes – no more, or the peas will lose their lovely bright green colour.

Slowly add the hot strained ham stock to the pea purée, beating well with a wooden spoon after each addition to get rid of any lumps of flour. When the stock is all added make sure that the bottom of the pan is clear of any lumps and simmer for 20 minutes.

Blanch the rest of the peas in boiling water for just 2 minutes and then take out and plunge into a bowl of iced water, to retain the colour. At this same time it is a good idea to skin the ham hock and take the meat from the bone. Carefully cut the flesh into fine dice. Mix this ham with half of the whole, blanched peas and keep to one side.

The soup is now cooked so take out the bunch of mint and add the remaining blanched peas (not those with the ham). Liquidise the soup and then I like to push it through a fine sieve or chinois.

Re-boil the soup gently, adding the cream and checking seasoning. Put the peas and ham into the soup and serve immediately.

(From *Brian Turner's Favourite British Recipes*, Headline, 2003)

Anton Mosimann

Mosimann's, Knightsbridge, London

Gazpacho

Serves 4

600g ripe tomatoes, skinned
1 green and 1 red pepper, seeded
1 small onion
½ garlic clove, peeled
½ cucumber, peeled
1 slice fresh bread, crusts removed, made into
breadcrumbs
1½ tbsp red wine vinegar
75ml Chicken Stock (see page 21)
60ml olive oil
a few fresh basil leaves
salt and pepper to taste

Roughly chop the tomatoes, peppers, onion, garlic and cucumber. Mix together with the crumbs in a large bowl or pan.

Mix the rest of the ingredients into the vegetables and breadcrumbs in the bowl, seasoning with salt and pepper to taste. Leave to marinate for 12 hours in the fridge.

After the ingredients have marinated, liquidise in batches to a fine purée, then push through a sieve or a food mill into serving bowls. Taste for seasoning, then chill.

To garnish, dice a little tomato, pepper and cucumber. Make some croûtons by cubing some bread, dousing generously in olive oil and baking in a hot oven (200ºC/Gas 6) until golden. Sprinkle all over the soup, or simply sprinkle with strips of fresh basil.

Bill Knott
Food writer

Ajo Blanco

This classic Spanish summer soup makes a change from gazpacho. It relies entirely on the freshness of the ingredients, so don't be tempted to use stale almonds, or ground almonds. If you can find fresh, wet almonds in season, so much the better. Use a virgin olive oil, preferably Andalusian, not a heavy, peppery oil, and muscatel (green) grapes, if you can find them.

Serves 4

1 thick slice day-old bread, crusts removed, cubed, soaked in water and squeezed out
225g unblanched almonds
4 garlic cloves
1 tbsp sherry vinegar
225ml olive oil
400ml ice-cold water
salt and white pepper to taste
24 white grapes, halved and seeded

After preparing the bread, blanch the almonds in boiling water for a minute or two, and slip them out of their skins. Blanch the garlic cloves for a minute too.

Put the almonds and garlic in a liquidiser with the bread, vinegar and oil and whizz until smooth. Gradually add the water: the soup should be the consistency of single cream, so adjust the quantity of water if necessary.

Season with salt and a little pepper.

Serve cold – over ice cubes, if you like – and garnish with the grapes.

Simon Haigh
Mallory Court, Royal Leamington Spa, Warwickshire

Soup of Raspberries and White Peaches

A soup often conjures up images of cold winter nights by the fire with crusty bread, so what better than to do something completely different – one for the end of the meal to refresh, and for when our fruits are at their best.

This dish comes from my days working with Raymond Blanc at Le Manoir aux Quat'Saisons where they served a similar recipe. Now we use an adapted version and when it's on our menu we have to keep a close eye on our chefs as they are often seen in the fridge with a spoon late on a warm summer's night, helping themselves!

Serves 4

350ml sweet white wine (the better the quality, the better the finished product)
250ml red wine
150g caster sugar
1 vanilla pod, split lengthways
2 large punnets raspberries (we like Blairgowrie)
1 large sprig fresh mint
juice of 1 lemon
2 whole ripe peaches, poached, skinned and cut into ⅛ths
crème fraîche or vanilla ice-cream, to serve (optional)

Bring the wines, sugar and vanilla to the boil. Put the raspberries into a bowl. When the wines have come to the boil, add the mint and pour over the raspberries. Taste for sweetness and add lemon juice if necessary.

Add the peach segments to the raspberries and chill until ice-cold. Remove the vanilla pod.

Serve in bowls as it is, or with a dollop of crème fraîche or a ball of vanilla ice-cream.

All Year

Many soup recipes can be made out of season – most chefs will use frozen peas and broad beans in the winter, for instance. Canned beans are also perfect in soup, as are canned tomatoes. Carrots, for example, though at their best in spring, can be bought all year round. Whilst buying produce in its natural prime is very satisfying, there are also times when the store cupboard can dictate what's on the menu.

Jamie Oliver

Fifteen, Shoreditch, London

Chickpea, Leek and Parmesan soup

Serves 4

2 medium leeks
15g butter
2 garlic cloves, chopped
1 handful fresh thyme, leaves picked
1 x 400g can chickpeas, drained and rinsed
600ml Chicken Stock (see page 21)
2 medium potatoes, peeled and chopped
salt and pepper to taste
extra virgin olive oil
freshly grated Parmesan

Trim the outside of the leeks back then cut off any coarse green tops and discard them. Cut the leeks in half lengthways and slice the halves into fine shreds. Put the chopped leeks in a colander and rinse thoroughly under running water, removing any dirt.

In a large saucepan, gently heat the butter and add the garlic, leeks and thyme leaves. Put the lid on the pot and slowly cook until soft without colouring.

Add the chickpeas to the leeks with the chicken stock and potatoes. Bring to the boil then simmer gently for half an hour or so or until the potatoes are well cooked. If the soup is too thick, loosen it with a little boiling water.

Break up the chickpeas and pieces of potato to thicken it slightly. Season carefully with sea salt and freshly ground black pepper, and pour into hot bowls. Top with a splash of olive oil and some grated Parmesan cheese.

Alastair Little
Tavola, Notting Hill, London

Potage Bonne Femme

Potage bonne femme is nothing more than a homely hot leek and potato soup but, puréed with judicious additions, it becomes a whole tribe of soups, some of which I detail below. Leek and potato has, since childhood, been my favourite soup, thus featuring strongly on my menus over the years.

Serves 4-6

2 medium leeks, trimmed of outer layers,
earthy ends and the darkest and damaged
part of the green
25g butter
3 medium potatoes, bakers or reds, peeled and
coarsely diced
salt and pepper to taste
1 litre Chicken Stock (see page 21) or water

Slice the leeks, put in a large bowl of warm water, and swirl them about to rinse off any dirt. Warm water is pretty vital here as leeks often contain sand or mud, neither of which is readily soluble in cold water. Using your hands or a spider lift the leeks out of their bath and into a colander. Rinse the bowl out thoroughly and repeat the process. If you simply pour the leeks from the bowl into the colander, all the carefully washed-out dirt will get back on them (the Roux brothers insist that washing leeks in warm water improves their flavour).

Melt the butter in a large solid-based saucepan and add the drained leeks. Sweat over a medium flame for 5 minutes or so; the leeks should partially collapse and glisten from their coating of butter, but should not take on any significant amount of colour. Add the diced potatoes and sweat for a further 5 minutes; they will start to stick after this time, a sure sign that their sweating period is over. Season judiciously with salt and pepper and add enough stock or water to cover the vegetables. Stir to make sure nothing is stuck to the bottom of the pan, turn

the heat up high and boil until the potatoes are tender, about 15-20 minutes. Allow to cool a little, then liquidise. Adjust seasoning and reheat if necessary before serving.

Homely leek and potato soup
This is my mother's version, and uses milk instead of stock. The soup is not puréed, and the milk looks a little grainy, but for satisfying flavour and all-round home-cooked, self-satisfied contentment, it's hard to beat. This soup is better if you include a larger proportion of the dark green parts of the leek, but make sure it's cut up into quite small pieces and cooked until tender.

Follow the basic recipe, substituting milk for stock. Do not boil the soup too fiercely as milk that gets too hot goes grainy and has a scalded flavour.

Leek and potato soup with mussels
Take 1kg of mussels, scrub and beard them. Rinse thoroughly and check for dead ones (any that seem too heavy or that are open and don't close when

firmly tapped). Boil these in 750ml water until open, then drain, reserving the water. When cool, shell them and put them in a bowl. Pour enough of the reserved liquor over them to cover.

Follow the basic recipe, substituting the mussel cooking liquor for stock. Do not liquidise the soup and do not add any salt (as the mussel liquor will be quite saline). Just before serving reheat the mussels and their covering liquor with the soup, taking care not to boil as this would toughen and shrink them.

Parsley soup.
Prepare the base recipe. Take a large bunch of Continental parsley and pick over it, losing the bigger stalks. Bring a large pan of water to a boil and blanch the parsley in this for 1 minute, then refresh by immersing in cold water. Add the cooked parsley to the soup and liquidise. Do not be too alarmed by the rather violent green colour of this soup. This was on the menu regularly at Frith Street with truffled crème fraîche.

Spinach soup
This is essentially the same as the parsley soup, substituting a 500g packet of spinach for the parsley. Blanch and refresh the spinach in exactly the same way as the parsley, add to the soup and liquidise. Spinach soup likes a little nutmeg in its make-up, which is best added when you are sweating the vegetables for the soup base.

Watercress soup
This was a rather trendy soup in Soho during the 1970s. Follow the recipe for the leek and potato soup base and add 4 bunches of watercress when it's finished. The watercress will wilt as you wait for the soup to cool down before liquidising.

Wild garlic soup
I used to be often spotted gathering these pungent leaves, a noted Soho specialty, at dawn in Soho Square. Wild garlic grows abundantly around Britain and a few leaves dropped into the leek and potato soup base about halfway through the cooking will, when liquidised, produce a delicious, if slightly anti-social soup.

Rocket soup
Rocket was the ultra trendy salad leaf of the mid 1990s. This soup paired with truffle oil is delicious. Proceed as for watercress soup. Certain more robust types of rocket may need the major stalks removed.

(From *Soho Cooking*, Ebury Press, 1999)

Heston Blumenthal
The Fat Duck, Bray, Berkshire

Latue de Mar

Serves 6-8

900ml Chicken Stock (see page 21)
900ml water
750g leeks, white parts only, thinly sliced
300g potatoes, peeled and thinly sliced
350g onions, finely chopped
1 bouquet garni
200g butter
1 cup latue de mar seaweed, soaked and rinsed
200ml double cream
salt and cayenne pepper to taste

Heat the chicken stock and water together, and reserve until needed.

In a saucepan over medium heat, sweat the leeks, potatoes, onions and bouquet garni in the butter until slightly soft, about 8 minutes.

Add the hot stock and water, and continue to simmer for 8 minutes until the potato is cooked. Remove the bouquet garni and discard.

Add the seaweed and double cream, and bring back to the boil.

Remove from the heat and blitz in a food processor. Pass through a fine chinois/sieve, and season with salt and cayenne pepper to taste.

Donna Hay

Food writer

Prawn, Lemongrass and Coconut soup

Serves 4

1 stalk lemongrass
2 tsp vegetable oil
1 tbsp red curry paste
1.2 litres Fish or Chicken stock (see pages 23 and 21)
400 ml coconut milk
4 large slices ginger
16 large raw prawns, shelled and cleaned, tails intact
2 tsp sugar
2 tbsp lime juice
1 tbsp fish sauce
2 tbsp coriander leaves

Cut slits in the lemongrass down to the root, keeping the stalk intact. Place the oil and curry paste in a large saucepan over medium-high heat and cook, stirring, for 1 minute. Add the lemongrass, stock, coconut milk and ginger and bring to a simmer. Simmer for 4 minutes.

Add the prawns and cook for 2 minutes. Stir in the sugar, lime juice and fish sauce.

Ladle the soup into bowls, discarding the lemongrass stalk and ginger. Top with the coriander leaves and serve.

Shaun Hill

The Merchant House, Ludlow, Shropshire

Fish Soup with Garlic, Saffron and Chilli

This soup is meant to be warm and spicy rather than vindaloo. The method is based on bourride, in that it is thickened with garlic mayonnaise, but the result is sharper and more citric.

The fish used can of course vary according to what suits and is available.

Serves 6

2 shallots, chopped
½ average-sized red pepper, seeded and diced
1 tbsp chopped celery
1 garlic clove, chopped
1 tbsp sunflower oil
5g saffron strands
1 bird's eye chilli, chopped
1 thin slice orange
1 litre Chicken Stock (see page 21)
100g brill fillet

100g red mullet fillet
100g white scallop meat

Garlic mayonnaise
1 tbsp lemon juice
1 tbsp Dijon mustard
2 egg yolks
1 garlic clove, crushed
salt and pepper to taste
50ml sunflower oil
50ml olive oil

First make the garlic mayonnaise by whisking together the lemon, mustard, egg yolks, garlic and seasoning and then slowly whisking in the oils.

For the soup, sweat the shallot, pepper, celery and garlic in the sunflower oil. Add the saffron, chilli and orange then the stock. Bring to the boil and simmer for a few moments.

Add the fish in the order in which it takes to cook – in this case the brill, followed by the red mullet, and then at the last moment the scallop.

Take the pan from the direct heat and remove the pieces of fish. Drain all the liquid into a blender along with the bits and pieces of vegetable and orange. Liquidise, adding the mayonnaise a spoonful at a time and stopping when the soup begins to thicken.

Pour the soup back on to the fish and warm through before serving.

Rick Stein

Seafood Restaurant, Padstow, Cornwall

Classic Fish Soup with Rouille and Croûtons

I love fish soup. I think it is one of those dishes like roast beef and Yorkshire pudding, which is so deeply satisfying that it has a special place in everyone's heart.

Serves 4

900g fish (such as gurnard, conger eel, dogfish, pouting, cod and grey mullet)
1.2 litres water
75ml olive oil
75g each roughly chopped onion, celery, leek and fennel
3 garlic cloves, sliced
juice of ½ orange, plus 1 piece pared orange zest
1 x 200g can chopped tomatoes
1 small red pepper, seeded and sliced
1 fresh bay leaf
1 sprig fresh thyme

a pinch of saffron
100g unpeeled North Atlantic prawns
a pinch of cayenne pepper
salt and pepper to taste

Croûtons
1 mini French baguette
1 garlic clove, peeled
olive oil for frying
25g (1oz) Parmesan, finely grated
2 tbsp rouille (can be found in jars)

Fillet the fish and use the bones with the water (and extra flavourings if you like) to make the fish stock (see page 23 for the method).

Heat the olive oil in a large pan, add the chopped vegetables and garlic and cook gently for 20 minutes until soft but not coloured. Add the orange zest, tomatoes, red pepper, bay leaf, thyme, saffron, prawns and fish fillets. Cook briskly for 2-3 minutes, then add the stock and orange juice, bring to the boil and simmer for 40 minutes.

Meanwhile, for the croûtons, thinly slice the mini baguette, rub with garlic, and fry in the olive oil until crisp and golden. Drain on kitchen paper.

Liquidise the soup, then pass it through a conical sieve, pressing out as much liquid as you can with the back of a ladle.

Return the soup to the heat and season to taste with the cayenne, salt and pepper.

To serve, ladle the soup into a warmed tureen and put the croûtons, Parmesan and rouille into separate dishes. Ladle the soup into warmed bowls and leave each person to spread some rouille on to the croûtons, float them on their soup and sprinkle it with some of the cheese.

Mary Contini

Valvona & Crolla Caffè Bar, Edinburgh

Pasta and Potato Soup/Pasta e Patate

At home, this soup was made religiously every Friday. We strictly kept the Catholic tradition of not eating meat on Fridays. This was no great hardship as pasta e patate is one of the most satisfying, comforting soups on the face of the earth. No matter what the priest says, no Italian mother would willingly deprive her family. In practice, the rule was obeyed in spirit only.

Serves 4

2 tbsp extra virgin olive oil
1 garlic clove
1 small piece peperoncino (dried chilli)
1 onion, very finely chopped
1 x 400g can Italian plum tomatoes
1.75 litres hot water
2 floury potatoes, peeled and diced
salt to taste
a handful of ditali rigate pasta (or small chunky pasta)
freshly grated Parmesan

Warm the oil in a large thick-bottomed saucepan and add the garlic and chilli. Add the chopped onion, stir and coat with the oil. Put the lid on and cook the onion slowly until it is soft and translucent. Don't let it burn.

Whizz the tomatoes in a liquidiser and, if you can be bothered, strain out the seeds by pressing the purée through a sieve. (You can use tomato passata instead.) Add the sieved tomatoes and 1 litre of the water to the onion, along with the potatoes and 1 tsp salt. Cover and cook for 30 minutes or so until the potatoes have softened. Remove the garlic.

Add the remaining water and the pasta. Stir and simmer for 10 minutes until the pasta is al dente. Check the seasoning, and serve in big warm bowls with plenty of freshly grated Parmesan.

I often poach a couple of eggs in this soup. When the pasta has started to cook, break 1-2 eggs on to the surface and let them poach gently as the pasta finishes cooking.

(From *Dear Francesca*, Ebury Press, 2002)

Ken Hom
Food writer

Tomato Ginger Soup

This soup is a year-round favourite of mine because tinned tomatoes are one of the few processed foods I use. Thus, this soup need not wait upon tomatoes in season. Use fresh tomatoes when they are available, and tinned tomatoes as the perfectly acceptable alternative. The fresh tomatoes, by the way, cook quickly and need little preparation. This is a refreshing soup and makes a sparkling starter. It reheats nicely. The recipe can easily be doubled, which makes it perfect for entertaining a number of friends.

Serves 4-6

450g fresh or tinned tomatoes
1.1 litres Chicken Stock (see page 21)
3 tbsp coarsely chopped fresh root ginger
1 tbsp light soy sauce
2 tsp chilli bean sauce
2 tsp caster sugar

If you are using fresh tomatoes, cut them in half horizontally. Squeeze the seeds out, coarsely chop the tomatoes and set aside.

Put the stock into a saucepan and bring to simmering point. Add the ginger, soy sauce, chilli bean sauce, sugar and tomatoes. Simmer for 2 minutes. Serve at once.

Note
For a South-East Asian touch, add 2 tbsp lemon juice. For hot summer days, serve this at room temperature.

Giorgio Locatelli
Locanda Locatelli, Mayfair, London

Zuppa Pavese
Soup with Bread and Poached Eggs

My grandmother used to cook me this soup whenever I felt a bit under the weather. I always thought of it as a special treat.

Serves 4

800ml Chicken Stock (see page 21)
salt to taste
50g butter
8 thick slices stale country bread
8 eggs
4 tbsp freshly grated Parmesan

Heat the stock, seasoning well with salt to taste.

Heat the butter in a large frying pan, add the bread and fry gently on both sides until crisp and golden (do this in batches if necessary).

Divide the slices between 4 deep soup plates and gently break an egg on top of each slice. Sprinkle over the grated Parmesan.

Slowly pour the hot stock into the soup plates, taking care not to pour it directly on top of the eggs.

Serve immediately.

(From *Tony and Giorgio*, 4th Estate, 2003)

Wah Cheong Soon
Yauatcha, Soho, London

Seafood Dumpling Consommé

This fabulous soup is classic dim-sum. To eat, break up the dumplings, releasing the individual flavours out into the broth. The amounts given make dough for approximately 50-60 dumpling skins. Attempting to make a smaller amount will make it difficult to get the consistency of the dough right. Freeze unused dough for later.

Serves 4

Fresh stock (makes 1 litre)
1 chicken carcass
1 leg of pork bone
4 litres cold water
salt to taste

Dumpling dough
300g plain extra-fine flour, plus extra for dusting/rolling
3 medium eggs
75ml cold water

Dumpling filling
75g raw king scallops, roughly chopped (without roe)
20g raw white crab meat
40g fresh bamboo shoots or tinned
20g fresh shiitake mushrooms, sliced

To serve
finely sliced fresh root ginger
black malt vinegar

To make the stock, place the chicken carcass and pork bone into a large pan of boiling water. Boil rapidly for 5 minutes and then discard the liquid. Pour the measured cold water into the pan with the bones and bring back to the boil. Add a good pinch of salt, turn the heat right down, cover the pan and gently simmer for approximately 4-6 hours or until the liquid has reduced to 1 litre. Leave to one side. (A fresh supermarket-bought chicken or vegetable stock can be used as a substitute.)

To make the dumpling dough, sift the flour into a large mixing bowl. Beat the eggs and slowly stir into the flour with a palette knife. Gradually stir in the water, reserving about 20ml, and start kneading on a floured surface. Knead firmly for 1-2 minutes or until the dough is smooth and pliable, adding the remaining water if necessary. Wrap the dough in clingfilm and chill for 15-20 minutes. After chilling, weigh out approximately 35g of the dough mixture.

On a lightly floured surface using both hands, roll out into a long cylindrical shape – about 2cm in diameter. Cut this roll into 4 equal pieces. Roll out each piece into a thin circle with a diameter of 8-10cm.

To make the dumpling filling, mix together all the ingredients in a bowl. Place a piece of dumpling skin in the palm of one hand and put a quarter of the filling in the middle. Fold the skin in half, creating a crescent shape. Seal the edges by squeezing the thumb and index finger together, pinching all the way around the curved edge to create a pleated effect.

To make the soup, heat the stock gently in a large pan until piping hot. Meanwhile, steam the dumplings for 4-5 minutes. Pour the stock into four soup bowls placing one dumpling in each. Serve immediately with side dishes of ginger and vinegar. Break up the dumpling using a soup spoon before eating to disperse the flavour.

Mark Edwards
Nobu Restaurant, Park Lane, London

Seafood Miso with Chorizo

This is a quick simple dish I sometimes make at home during winter. It's more of a stew than a soup, combining the warming hearty properties of miso soup with a western twist.

Serves 4

Dashi
1.5 litres water
5cm piece dried kombu (dried kelp)
25g dried bonito flakes

Miso soup
125g white miso paste
2 garlic cloves, finely chopped
50g onions, sliced
olive oil
100g chorizo (I like it spicy), sliced
50g celery, sliced
100g potatoes, peeled and diced
4 shrimps, peeled

4 large scallops
100g salmon, cut into 4
75g squid or cuttlefish
50g Chinese cabbage, sliced
50g fresh spinach
a bunch of celery leaves
freshly ground black pepper
a knob of butter (optional)

To serve
2 spring onions, finely shredded
togarashi (shichimi, Japanese seven-spice seasoning)

First make the dashi by bringing the water and kombu to a gentle boil, then remove from the heat. Add the bonito flakes and leave to cool, then strain.

Heat up the dashi and whisk in the miso paste, taking care not to let the mixture boil otherwise it will become bitter.

In a separate, large saucepan, gently sweat the garlic and sliced onion in a little olive oil, then add the chorizo and celery (not the celery leaves), and continue to sweat for a further 5 minutes.

Strain the miso soup on to the onions and chorizo and add the potatoes. Bring up to barely a simmer and cook for around 20 minutes or until the potatoes are just cooked.

Next add all the seafood and the cabbage and bring back to a very gentle simmer. Add the spinach and celery leaves and cook for a further 3 minutes. Season with freshly ground black pepper and stir in a good knob of butter to enrich the soup if desired.

Serve the soup in large bowls with Japanese togarashi on the side. Sprinkle with the sliced spring onions.

Peter Gordon

Providores, Marylebone, London

Garlic, Chorizo and Chickpea Broth with Egg Noodles

The hearty flavour of pimentón-flavoured chorizo really lifts this hearty soup, and the 'noodles' are really easy to make.

Serves 6-8

12 garlic cloves, halved
80ml extra virgin olive oil
200g chorizo sausage
2 large red onions, diced
1 tbsp fresh rosemary leaves, roughly chopped
1 tbsp fresh oregano leaves, roughly chopped
600g canned chickpeas, drained and rinsed
2 bay leaves
finely grated zest and juice of 1 lemon
1 litre Chicken or Vegetable Stock (see pages 21 or 19)

Noodles
1 egg
2 tsp cold water
2 pinches salt
1 tsp olive oil

Cook the garlic in the oil in a very small pan over a very gentle heat, stirring occasionally, until soft and golden (about 20 minutes). Remove with a slotted spoon. Peel any casing from the chorizo and slice half into thin discs, then fry until cooked in the same oil that you cooked the garlic in. Remove with a slotted spoon and set aside. Cut the remaining chorizo into small cubes.

Transfer the oil to a larger pot. Add the onions, diced chorizo, rosemary and oregano, and fry until they begin to caramelise. Add the caramelised garlic, the chickpeas, bay leaves, lemon zest and stock and bring to the boil. Simmer for 30 minutes.

Make the noodles while the soup is cooking. Lightly beat together the egg, water and salt. Heat a 24cm non-stick pan and brush with a few drops of oil. Drizzle in the egg mixture so it covers the base of the pan. Cook over a moderate heat until just set. Tip on to a board, roll up and cut into 1cm slices. Unroll into 'noodles'.

Taste the broth for seasoning and stir in the lemon juice. Ladle into bowls and serve with the egg noodles and chorizo discs scattered on top.

(From A World in My Kitchen, Moa Beckett, Hodder, 2003)

David Thompson
Nahm, Halkin Hotel, Knightsbridge, London

Geng Jeut Bachor
Clear Soup of Minced Pork and Celery

Either chicken or prawn mince can be used – or indeed, if you are vegetarian, you can omit the meat and increase the mushrooms.

Serves 4-6

900ml Chicken Stock (see page 21)
a pinch of salt
a pinch of white sugar
1-2 tbsp light soy sauce
a little oyster sauce
100g pork, coarsely minced with little garlic, ginger and salt
20g Asian celery or spring onions, cut into 2cm lengths

a few cloud ear mushrooms, torn into bite-sized pieces (see below)
a piece of silken beancurd
minced deep-fried garlic (see below)
1 tbsp coriander leaves
a pinch of ground white pepper

Bring the stock to the boil, and season with salt, sugar, light soy and oyster sauce. Add the pork mince, stirring to prevent the meat clumping. Do not overcook the mince – a moment or two is sufficient, otherwise it will toughen and become oily. Add the celery, cloud ear mushrooms and beancurd. Serve sprinkled with the deep-fried garlic, coriander and pepper.

Deep-fried Garlic/Gratiam Jiaw
For garlic to deep-fry successfully, a certain amount needs to be fried – usually at least a handful of cloves – otherwise it is difficult to control the cooking, and it can burn easily and all too quickly. Slice the garlic lengthwise into thin, even slices. It is important to slice the garlic lengthwise, so that the slices deep-fry evenly and crisply, rather than becoming knotted discs. The slices should also be as fine as possible – almost paper-thin – so that they cook quickly, evenly and become crispy and golden; if they are too thick, the edges will burn

while the inside remains undercooked.

Heat vegetable oil in a wok until moderately hot, then add garlic and reduce the heat a little. Deep-fry, stirring constantly with tongs. When the garlic starts to lose its sharp peppery aroma and smells nutty, and starts to turn amber and then a light honey-gold, remove it from the oil. Drain and spread out on absorbent paper to cool. Pass the oil through a sieve to collect any scraps before re-use; the garlic-infused oil can be used for deep-frying or stir-frying.

The garlic will keep for 2-3 days in an airtight container.

Note
Cloud ears have a delicate flavour that absorbs the taste of more strongly flavoured ingredients in cooking. They are sold fresh and dried in Asian stores.

George Lewis
Graphic designer, Soup Kitchen

Finn's Soup

When I left home my mother gave me a copy of Katharine Whitehorn's *Cooking in a Bedsitter*, a truly great cookbook. It is very usefully divided into two sections:

Part One: Cooking to Stay Alive
Part Two: Cooking to Impress

which pretty much encompassed my requirements at the time. On soup, Katharine says this, 'It is simply not worthwhile making your own soup in a bedsitter. You cannot start monkeying around with stock and chicken carcasses, and there are dozens of excellent packet, tinned, condensed and cube soups on the market to choose from.'

It just so happens that my happiest memory of soup is eating a bowl of Heinz tomato soup with a poached egg in it at my friend Finn's house in Wales. Here's my humble addition to this collection.

Serves 2

1 large can Heinz tomato soup
4 free-range eggs

Garnish
crème fraîche
butter
Worcestershire sauce
grated cheese

The temptation here is to heat the soup as fast as you can, removing it from the heat just as you achieve the look of orange cappuccino. However, it does pay to follow the instructions on the can, heating slowly, stirring occasionally and not letting it boil.

Meanwhile poach your egg. I do mine in a pan of water with a dash of vinegar in it but each to his own. Garnish and serve with toast. Bob's your uncle.

Chris Galvin

Wolseley, Mayfair, London

Chicken Soup with Dumplings

Serves 4

1kg chicken bones
giblets from 2 chickens
1 boiling fowl
1 onion, quartered
1 large carrot, peeled and cut in half lengthways
1 large celery stalk, cut in half
1 leek, washed and roughly chopped
a small pinch of saffron strands
1 bouquet garni
5 litres water
salt to taste
15g white peppercorns, crushed

Dumplings or matzo balls
2 eggs, separated
30g fine matzo meal
1 tsp chopped fresh parsley
a few drops of chicken fat

Garnish
6 young leeks, cooked in the stock and cut into 1cm pieces
6 fingerling carrots, cooked in the stock and sliced
shredded meat from the boiling fowl

Place all of the soup ingredients, apart from the peppercorns, into the cold water in a large stockpot, bring to the boil and skim. Allow to gently boil (at a tremble) for 2 hours, skimming any impurities from the stock. Add the crushed peppercorns for the last 30 minutes, taste, season and remove from the heat. Allow to stand for a further 30 minutes.

Carefully remove the boiling fowl and reserve, then pass the stock through a fine chinois/strainer. The secret of a clear bouillon is to ladle the stock out carefully, avoiding mixing in too much fat at this point. If not using immediately, cool as quickly as possible.

Meanwhile, for the dumplings, beat the egg whites to soft peaks. Stir the yolks into the matzo meal. Fold the whites into the mixture gently, then add the parsley and a little fat to flavour, and finally salt to taste. Roll into marble-sized balls and poach in boiling water for 15 minutes until they have all floated to the surface and feel light in relation to size. (The secret to producing light matzo balls is

working the mixture for as short a time as possible and as lightly as one can.)

When the boiling fowl is cool, pick off the meat. Shred and reserve for the garnish.

To serve, heat the soup through, then add the sliced carrot and leek, then the shredded chicken. Add the matzo balls and serve.

John Torode
Smiths of Smithfield, Clerkenwell, London

Stracciatella with Fresh Chicken

This soup was served in Australian restaurants in the late 1980s when the chef was too lazy to make a slow-cooked soup for the daily menu, or an underling forgot. It is, however, one of the most delicious and simple soups you could ever eat, even easier now that fresh stocks are readily available on the supermarket shelves, if you don't want to make your own. And, if push comes to shove, you can use a stock cube. The important thing with this soup is to take it from the heat as soon as you have added the egg mix or it will overcook. The egg, Parmesan and parsley will float to the top like a raft, leaving the rich stock and chunks of chicken sitting below.

Serves 6

1.5 litres Chicken Stock (see page 21)
3 skinless chicken breasts, cut into strips
4 eggs
60g Parmesan, freshly grated
a good handful of parsley, finely chopped
ground black pepper to taste

Place a suitable saucepan over a high heat, pour in the stock and bring to the boil. Add the chicken to the boiling stock, and cook for 5 minutes.

Beat the eggs with the cheese, chopped parsley and black pepper.

Pour the egg mix into the boiling liquid and remove from the heat immediately.

Serve in 6 large bowls, with crusty bread and butter or olive oil.

Nick Nairn

Chef and Restaurateur

Carrot, Ginger and Honey Soup

Fabby colour. Easy to make. Tastes great. Cheap. What more could you want from a soup?

Serves 6

2 tbsp olive oil
150g onion, thinly sliced
20g fresh root ginger, peeled
600g carrots, peeled and grated
1 tbsp clear honey
juice of 1 lemon
2 tsp Maldon salt
5 turns freshly ground black pepper
900ml boiling water

Heat the olive oil in a large saucepan. Add the onions and stir well to coat. Don't let the onions go brown.

Using the flat edge of a heavy knife, crush the ginger (this releases the oil). Add to the onions and let them sweat for 10 minutes.

Now add the grated carrot, honey, lemon juice, salt and pepper, and stir well. Pour in the boiling water and bring to the boil. Simmer for 45 minutes. You may have to add a little more water during this time to allow for evaporation.

Remove the pan from the heat and liquidise the contents (with a hand blender or in the liquidiser) until smooth and creamy.

Check the seasoning and serve.

If you are making the soup ahead and you want to freeze it, allow the soup to cool before pouring it into a sealable tub and putting it into the freezer. If you're not freezing it, the soup will keep well for up to three days

Henry Harris
Racine, Knightsbridge, London

Cannellini Bean and Smoked Haddock Soup

Soups should come from a pan and not a carton or can. Using cooked beans saves on preparation time but you can soak some dried beans in water overnight if you would like and then cook for an hour or two in boiling water until tender. I have made this soup from start to finish in 20 minutes. Use a powerful blender such as a KitchenAid for that velvety smooth restaurant finish.

Serves 4

a knob of butter
2 large onions, sliced
1 x 400g cannellini/haricot beans,
drained and rinsed
800ml light Chicken Stock (see page 21)
a pinch of saffron, soaked in hot water
250ml whipping cream
250g smoked haddock, skin and bones discarded
Tabasco sauce

Melt the butter in a heavy saucepan, add the onions and cook until soft. Add the beans, stock, saffron and cream and bring to a gentle simmer. Add the haddock and cook for 5–10 minutes. Transfer in small batches to a powerful liquidiser and blitz until smooth. Pass it though a fine sieve and pour it into a clean pan.

Reheat and then adjust the seasoning, adding a good warming splash of Tabasco. Garnish with fingers of toasted rustic bread.

Claudia Roden
Food writer

Yoghurt Soup with Rice

Apart from the pleasure it gives, soup represents to me homely comfort food, affection and nurture. In this Turkish soup, the egg yolk and flour prevent the yoghurt from curdling. The rice is best cooked separately and added in at the end as it gets bloated and mushy if left in the soup too long.

Serves 6

100g basmati rice
salt and pepper to taste
1.2 litres Chicken Stock (see page 21, but you may use 2 stock cubes)
450g thick strained yoghurt
2 tbsp plain flour
2 egg yolks
1½ tbsp dried mint
1 x 400g can chickpeas, drained and rinsed (optional)
30g butter or 2 tbsp olive oil (optional)
2 tsp paprika (optional)

Cook the rice in boiling salted water until tender, and drain.

Bring the chicken stock to the boil in a large pan.

In a bowl beat the yoghurt with the flour and egg yolks until blended, then add the mint, salt and pepper. Pour this into the stock, stirring vigorously. Continue to stir, over a very low heat, until the soup thickens slightly.

Before serving, add the rice and chickpeas (if using) and heat through. If you like, heat the butter or olive oil, stir in the paprika and dribble a little of this over each serving.

Variations
A pinch of saffron strands steeped in 2 tbsp hot water may be added instead of the butter and paprika at the end.

An Iranian version adds a ¼ tsp of turmeric and a variety of chopped herbs, including parsley, tarragon and chives, as well as shredded spinach.

Theodore Kyriakou
Real Greek, Hoxton, London

Chicken Avgolemono Soup

This is a soup where Jewish mothers meet Greek Orthodox mothers. It has a legendary reputation for being the best hangover cure (as well as being an amazing cure for a cold) and is a classic greek recipe. Enjoy!

Serves 4

2 litres water
1kg leafy carrots, peeled and left whole
4 bay leaves
1 x 2kg chicken
½ kg leeks, washed, trimmed of green parts and cut in half horizontally, if very long)
2 bunches spring onions, trimmed, washed and left whole
120g Greek short-grain rice
3 medium eggs, separated

juice of 2 lemons
salt and pepper to taste

Put the water into a large pot and add the carrots and bay leaves. Bring to boiling point and cook for 15 minutes. Turn the heat down and submerge the whole chicken. Leave to simmer with the lid on for 45 minutes.

Add the leeks and spring onions and keep simmering for a further 20 minutes.

Remove the cooked chicken and the vegetables with a slotted spoon and keep them warm. Carve the chicken into portions and cut up the vegetables.

Add the rice to the broth, of which there should be approximately 1.5 litres, and stir. Leave to simmer for 10 minutes, or until the rice is almost cooked.

To finish thickening the soup, firstly whisk the egg whites until they peak in a mixing bowl. Add a quarter of the broth to the bowl, a little at a time, and fold in, together with the lemon juice and, finally, the egg yolks.

Reduce the heat under the soup to a minimum and stir the contents of the mixing bowl back in the bulk of the soup. Keep stirring until the soup thickens. Do not let the soup boil or it will curdle. Season with salt and pepper.

The soup can be eaten either alongside the chicken and vegetables, or on its own as a first course. The chicken and vegetables should be eaten at room temperature.

(From *Real Greek Food* by Theodore Kyriakou and Charles Campion, Pavilion, 2000)

Scott Webster
Chef

Hot Chocolate Soup and Vanilla Pepper Ice-cream

Serves 6 (or a slightly greedier 4)

100g milk chocolate, broken into bits
50g dark chocolate (70% or more cocoa solids
is best), broken into bits
140g butter
80g cocoa powder
200g caster sugar
80g honey
80g egg yolks
130ml crème fraîche
120g egg whites

Ice-cream
375ml milk
375ml double cream
150g caster sugar
1 vanilla pod
200g egg yolks
10g cracked black peppercorns

For the ice-cream, bring the milk, cream, sugar and vanilla pod to the boil in a heavy-bottomed saucepan. Pour into the egg yolks in a bowl, whisking continuously to form a paste. Pour back into the pan and stir until thick. Do not allow to boil or you will have scrambled eggs; keep stirring all the time whilst it is thickening. Pour through a strainer and allow to cool on an ice bath. Fold in the black pepper to taste. Some like it hot! Place in an ice-cream machine and churn, or if you do not have an ice-cream machine, put in the deep freeze and stir at regular intervals until it is frozen.

Preheat the oven to 150ºC/Gas 2.

For the 'soup', melt the chocolate and butter over a bain-marie (or in a microwave), then mix with the cocoa powder, half the sugar, the honey, egg yolks and crème fraîche into a smooth paste. Mix a little of the liquid chocolate into the cocoa powder first, to a smooth paste, and then mix in with the rest of the ingredients, to avoid cocoa lumps.

Whip the egg whites up until they start forming peaks. Add the remaining sugar and carry on whisking until the whites hold their shape. Fold the egg white mixture into the chocolate sauce. Put in a greased 1.2 litre soufflé dish, and bake in the preheated oven for 10 minutes.

When serving the soup you will need to put it in a preheated oven at 180ºC/Gas 4 for 3 minutes and serve the pepper ice-cream on the side.

Bread

Bread

Bread in this country has come an awfully long way in the last decade or so. Before we were lucky to get a choice between a crusty white cottage loaf and a granary. Mostly we opted for sliced from the supermarket. But thankfully opinions, and standards, have changed. Nowadays a whole host of companies have cropped up around the country that make sourdoughs, ciabattas, focaccias, rye bread, breads studded with nuts and fruit, breads in baguettes, plaits, rosettes and other enticing shapes. Village bakeries that were threatened by closure from the competition of ever-expanding supermarket networks have suddenly found their fan base is growing. People have cottoned on that bread without preservatives may not last as long, but sure does taste good. Hooray for proper freshly baked bread!

One can go on about bread for a long time. It is a seemingly endless topic. You can have a bread starter living in your fridge alongside your cheese and eggs, happily breeding wild yeasts that make an exceptionally tasty loaf. If you feel, after reading this book, that your soups are worthy of a similarly splendid crust, than we recommend you delve through some ground-breaking books such as Baker & Spice's *Baking with Passion* by Dan Lepard and Richard Whittington, or Carol Field's *The Italian Baker*, or the blissfully easy to use *Ballymaloe Bread Book*.

If, in the meantime, you laugh in the face of buying your bread and you fancy a challenge, but are not quite ready to become a baker extraordinaire, we have included a few simple recipes for you to accompany your favourite soup.

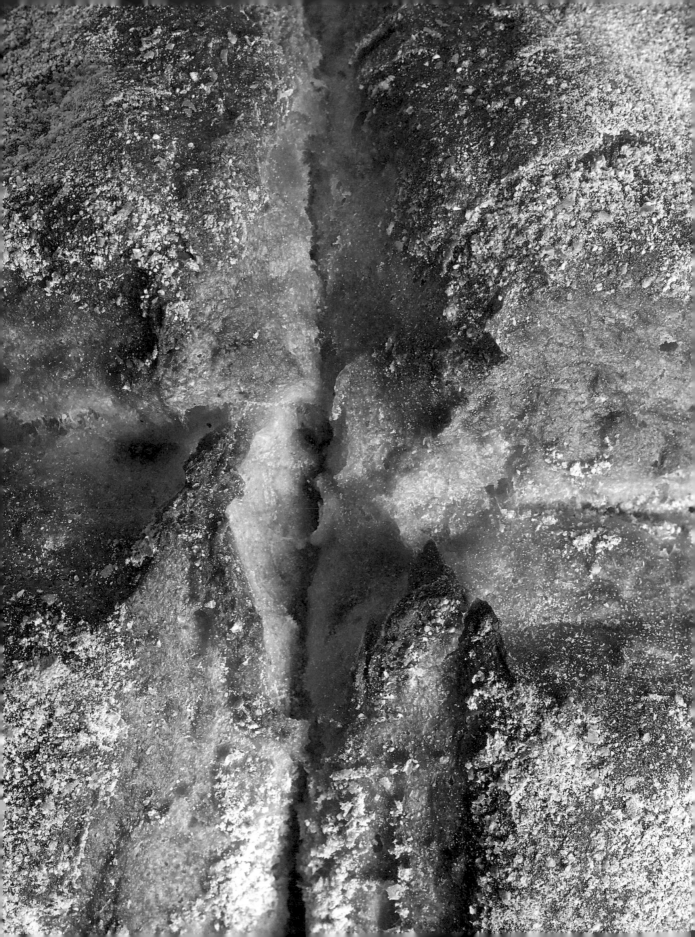

Irish Soda Bread

The easiest of them all, with none of that hard kneading involved. The important thing to note in soda bread is to handle the dough as little as possible. It literally takes a few minutes to make and then half an hour to bake. Add in chopped olives, caramelised onions, chopped herbs, cheese toppings or anything else to the basic dough recipe if you want to ring the changes.

Makes 1 loaf

375g white flour
75g wholemeal flour
1 level tsp salt, granular not flaky
1 level tsp baking soda
350-410ml buttermilk

Preheat the oven to 230ºC/Gas 8.

Sieve the dry ingredients into a bowl, and make a well in the centre. Now tip in most of the buttermilk and with one hand mix quickly and deftly, using a broad circular motion. The mixture should be soft, but not too sticky and sloppy. When it comes together tip it out on to a floured work surface.

It's now crucial to wash your hands and dry them. Flour your hands and pat the bread into a round, tidy shape and flip over gently on to a floured baking tray. Make a cross across the top and bake in the hot oven for 15 minutes, then turn down the oven to 200ºC /Gas 6 for another 20-30 minutes until cooked. It should sound hollow when tapped on the bottom. This recipe makes very good scones too, if you want each of your guests to have one; and they are quick to cook too.

NB As with all bread, try to avoid leaping into it, straight from the oven. If it is cut whilst still warm the steam escapes and the bread loses its lovely texture and becomes doughy.

Naan Bread

This is a fragrant, inviting bread adapted from a Maddhur Jaffrey recipe. Whilst most naan breads are traditionally cooked on the walls of clay ovens, this one can be heated in the oven or under the grill.

Makes 6 naans

150ml warm milk
2 tsp caster sugar
2 tsp dried yeast
450g plain flour
½ tsp salt, granular not flaky
1 tsp baking powder
2 tbsp vegetable oil
150g plain yoghurt, lightly beaten
1 large egg, beaten
garnish of choice (optional, see below)

Put the milk in a bowl with 1 tsp of the sugar and the yeast. Set aside for 15 minutes to activate and become frothy. Sift the flour, salt and baking powder into a large bowl and make a well in the centre. Add the rest of the sugar, the yeast liquid, vegetable oil, yoghurt and egg. Mix thoroughly until the dough comes together.

Tip on to a clean work surface and knead for 10 minutes, until it becomes smooth and shiny. Form the dough into a ball and oil it lightly with some extra vegetable oil. Put in a large bowl, cover with a tea-towel, and leave somewhere warm to double in size, about an hour.

Preheat the oven to its highest setting and put in a heavy baking tray to heat through. Preheat the grill to its highest setting.

Rescue the dough and divide into 6 balls. Cover 5 and with the remaining one, slap it down and push into a naan shape with your fingers. Flip it down on to the hot baking tray and bake for 3 minutes, whereupon it will puff up beautifully. If you like at this stage you can top the bread with garlic butter or coriander butter or, when you are shaping it, you can mix the dough with fillings of pine nuts, poppy seeds, raisins, spring onions, spinach. Then quickly put the naan under the hot grill for a further minute and lightly brown. Once it is cooked keep in a warm tea-towel whilst you cook the other 5. Serve hot.

Brown Bread

This is a delicious, easy, nutty loaf that goes very well with butter and a mature Cheddar, quite apart from being perfect with soup.

Makes 1 loaf

400g wholemeal flour
50g strong white flour
1 tsp salt, granular not flaky
1 tsp black treacle
150ml lukewarm water, plus 300ml more
30g fresh yeast, or 1 sachet dried yeast
pumpkin seeds to top

Preheat the oven to 230ºC/Gas 8, and grease a 13 x 20cm loaf tin.

Sieve the flours and salt into a bowl and leave in a warm place. In a small bowl mix the treacle and the 150ml water, then crumble in the yeast. It is important that the temperature of the water is right. Too hot, and the heat will kill the yeast; too cold, and it will not get it going. Leave the yeast water in a warm place to come to life for 15 minutes. Once it has started looking creamy and bubbling a little, pour it along with the rest of the water into the flour to make a fairly wet dough. You should not be able to knead it.

Pour into the prepared tin and cover with the seeds. Leave to rise with a damp tea-towel on top, and after 20 minutes or so the loaf will have risen to twice its original size. Remove the cloth and pop into the oven for about 40 minutes. Take out the loaf from the tin and put back in the oven for another 10 minutes to cut a nice crust.

Acknowledgements

The prelude to Soup Kitchen was a design project called Can of Gold. The brainchild of Marcel Wanders, a Dutch designer with a vision, Can of Gold used the simple idea of gilding Campbell's soup cans in 24-carat gold to raise money for local homeless charities (the project had already successfully run in Hamburg, Washington and Sydney). Annabel was working on Can of Gold in London in conjunction with amazing furniture retailer Noel Hennessy Furniture. At the same time Thomasina was working around the corner at Villandry. When Annabel approached Villandry to support Can of Gold, she and Tommi met and hit it off and Annabel made the mistake of mentioning a soup book idea.

A huge thank you is due to all those involved in supporting Can of Gold, including: Martha Greene at Villandry, Swarovski, The Royal Netherlands Embassy, Philip Treacy, Paul Smith and Sophie Mill, No.5 Maddox Street, Ripping Image, Gilly Booth, the genius Marcel Wanders, and of course the wonderful, bow-tied Noel Hennessy and his Mrs Rose-Marie, without whom none of this would have happened.

There are so many people to thank for the book but space allows mainly a long list of names. However, two major stars stand out: our photographer Richard Learoyd and our graphic designer George Lewis (both of whom also worked on the Can of Gold project). Their creative genius speaks for itself and this book would be nothing without their ideas and relentless energy and hard work. Time and time again, it has been the visuals which have inspired people to take the book seriously and come on board. Richard, thank you for the Eccles cakes at St John's, thank you for taking time to call us every week for updates and to check on our mental health, thank you for having such a clear vision for the book from allotments to graph paper and for the endless hours you've put in (the 4am trip to Billingsgate was nothing short of heroic). Thank you for never quibbling about costs, about the endless prints and Alan's time and for always being so supportive and enthusiastic about the book in the midst of your massive workload and paternity leave. You have been a legend. Nying nying. Thank you too to Kate, Josephine and Tom for being a part of the team. George, thank you for all the extras you have done for us from logos to AIs. Thank you for never being a prima donna and for embracing whatever this book has demanded, be it washing up or biking across London in the rain to buy a copy of Quark. Thank you for being so patient and the voice of calm. And especially thank you for never being ashamed to come to meetings at Carluccio's clad entirely in bright Lycra and those tappy cycling shoes and for juggling two more females in your life between school runs and the Bar. Thank you too to Sibby, Roma and Jude.

Thank you to Hugh Fearnley-Whittingstall, for agreeing to help us when there was no earthly reason to (and not backing out as we increasingly demanded publicity time, lunch at Andrew Edmonds AND that introduction). Thank you for introducing us to the wonderful Antony Topping at Greene and Heaton. Antony, thank you for being so amazingly level-headed, for negotiating the best possible contract for the charities at the same time as being such an oasis of calm. Pete and Jo from Sign Associates, thank you for catching our rainbow, jumping on board and building our website for Soup Kitchen. McDermott Will and Emery, thank you for giving us the time and legal brilliance of Kate Learoyd, Duncan Curley and Rohan Massey. It has been a pleasure to work with your professional team. Thank you to our accountant Steve. To Denise at HarperCollins, thank you for your professionalism and foresight and for sharing our enthusiasm so early on and for 'getting' what we were banging on about.

Thank you to our wonderful partners: Steve Osborne at Maldon Salt and Faith and Niall McArthur at EAT. Thank you for sharing and supporting our vision so generously.

To every chef (please see full list to right) and every PA, agent, secretary, publicist and PR company who has helped to get us the recipes in this book we send enormous thanks.

Plus: Abigail Bryans, Alan Cook, Ali Cargill, all the friends who have bought us lunch over the past year, Bill Knott (for endless generosity of spirit and food knowledge), Campbell Clark (for being there right at the start when we most needed help), Carluccio's, Cherie Colman, Cheryl Cohen, Chloe Lilley, Clare Griffin, Clemente Cavigioli, Damien Fraser, Daron, Nicky and Tess, Duncan Cargill, Eleanor Kinloch, Emma Bridgewater, Galton and Tracy Blackiston, Gareth Williams, Gilly Booth, Gray Poehnell, Howard de Walden Estates, Hugo Lawrence, Ion Mills, Jasper Morrison, Jessica Gruber (and her duck), Jessica Killick, Jim and Rita Houston, John and Jenny Peters, John Loughlin, John Bird and The Big Issue, Jon Jo and Bart, Julie Reese, Karin Krautgartner, Kate Hume, Lawrence Barber, Lincoln and Trish Seligman (and their cleaning lady), Linda Yau, Louise-Anne Comeau, Mark Bond, Matthew Rice, Michael Salmon, Mission, Naomi Hancock, Neal's Yard, Nicky SJ, Nigel and Sandra Worthington from Norwich City FC, Nu-nu Yee, Oliver Peyton, Patricia Michelson and Sarah at La Fromagerie, Paul Torjussen and Ion Mills at Southbank Publishing, Rebecca Hall, Ruth Donoghue, Sally Watson, Sarah Boardman, Sarah Miller, Sebastian Conran, Sebastiano at Primal Soup, Steven Bateman at Howard de Walden Estates, Serena Colchester, Serena Freeland, Sophie Mill, Stephen Bateman, Stuart Barber, Susan Duffy, The Conran Shop, Thomas Viner, Tom Parker-Bowles, Vanessa Parr, Vivienne Taylor, Wendy Hawk, Will Andrews.

Thank you to the following chefs and food writers who contributed recipes to this collection:

Antony Worrall Thompson, Daniel Woodhouse, Ian Wood, Marco Pierre White, Scott Webster, Marcel Wanders, Brian Turner, Andrew Turner, Eric Treuille, John Torode, Mitchell Tonks, Chee Hwee Tong, David Thompson, Jamie Thewes, Rick Stein, Shirley Spear, Wah Cheong Soon, Delia Smith, Germain Schwab, Camilla Schneiderman, Nino Sassu, Michel Roux, Claudia Roden, Gary Rhodes, Gordon Ramsay, Alfred Prasad, Bruce Poole, Aaron Patterson, Jamie Oliver, Ben O'Donoghue, Nick Nairn, Anton Mosimann, Mohammed Ourad, Dave Miney, Patricia Michelson, Faith MacArthur, Peter Lute, Giorgio Locatelli, Alastair Little, Prue Leith, Rowley Leigh, Jeremy Lee, Richard Learoyd, Nigella Lawson, Nico Ladenis, Theodore Kyriakou, Atul Kochar, Bill Knott, Ken Hom, Mark Hix, Shaun Hill, Fergus Henderson, Donna Hay, Angela Hartnett, Sam Hart, Henry Harris, Ainsley Harriott, Anna Hansen, Simon Haigh, Richard Guest, Sophie Grigson, Rose Gray and Ruth Rogers, Graham Grafton, Peter Gordon, Skye Gyngell, Andre Garrett, Chris Galvin, Hugh Fearnley-Whittingstall, David Eyre, David Everitt-Matthias, Steve Evenett-Watts, Mark Edwards, Jill Dupleix, Roz Denny, Tamasin Day-Lewis, Richard Corrigan, Mary Contini, Tom Conran, Terence Conran, Sophie Conran, Sally Clarke, Sam and Sam Clark, Maxine Clark, Antonio Carluccio, Charles Campion, John Campbell, Michael Caines, Adam Byatt, Martin Burge, Mark Broadbent, Heston Blumenthal, Raymond Blanc, Galton Blackiston, Herbert Berger, Jeff Baker, Pascal Aussignac, Darina Allen, Tom Aikens.

Restaurant contacts

Where a chef has more than one restaurant or shop we have given details of their flagship location only.

1880   27-33 Harrington Gardens London SW7 4JX   020 7244 5555
1 Lombard Street   1 Lombard Street London EC3V 9AA   020 7929 6611
Almeida   30 Almeida Street London N1 1TD   020 7354 4777
Assaggi   39 Chepstow Place, Notting Hill London W2 4TS   020 7792 5501
Atlantic Bar and Grill   20 Glasshouse Street London W1B 5DJ   0871 332 4219
Ballymaloe   Shanagarry, Midleton, County Cork Ireland   00 353 21 464 6785
Barnsley House   Barnsley, Cirencester Gloucestershire GL7 5EE   01285 740 000
Benares   12a Berkeley Square London W1J 6BS   020 7629 8886
Bluebird Dining Room   350 Kings Road London SW3 5UU   020 7559 1129
Blueprint Café   Design Museum, 28 Shad Thames London SE1 2YD   020 7378 7031
Books for Cooks   4 Blenheim Crescent London W11 1NN   020 7221 1992
Brian Turner   Mayfair Millennium Hotel, 44 Grosvenor Square London W1K 2HP   020 7596 3444
Champignon Sauvage   24-26 Suffolk Road, Cheltenham Gloucestershire GL50 2AQ   01242 573449
Chez Bruce   2 Bellevue Road, Wandsworth Common London SW17 7EG   020 8672 0114
Clarke's   124 Kensington Church Street London W8 4BH   020 7221 9225
Club Gascon   57 West Smithfield London EC1A 9DS   020 7796 0600
Deca   23 Conduit Street London W1S 2XS   020 7493 7070
Divertimenti   33-34 Marylebone High Street London W1U 4BP   020 7935 0689
EAT   www.eatcafe.com   020 7636 8309
Eyre Brothers   70 Leonard Street London EC2A 4QX   020 7613 5346
Fifteen   15 Westland Place London N1 7LP   0871 330 1515
Fino   33 Charlotte Street London W1T 1RR   020 7813 8010
FishWorks   (and other locations)   6 Green Street Bath BA1 2JY
Gidleigh Park   Chagford Devon TQ13 8HH   01647 432 367
Gordon Ramsay at Claridges   Claridge's Hotel, Brook Street London W1S 1EY   020 7499 0099
Gordon Ramsay at Royal Hospital Road   68 Royal Hospital Road, Chelsea London SW3 4HP   020 7352 4441
Hakkasan   8 Hanway Place London W1T 1HB   020 7927 7000
Hambleton Hall   Hambleton, Oakham Rutland LE15 8TH   01572 756 991
Hoxton Apprentice   16 Hoxton Square London N1 6NT   020 7749 2828
J. Sheekey   28-32 St Martins Court London WC2N 4AL   020 7240 2565
Kensington Place   201-209 Kensington Church St London W8 7LX   020 7727 3184
La Fromagerie   2-4 Moxon Street London W1U 4EW   020 7935 0341
Le Gavroche   43 Upper Brook Street London W1K 7QR   020 7408 0881
Le Manoir aux Quat' Saisons   Church Road, Great Milton Oxford OX44 7PD   01844 278 881
Lindsay House   21 Romilly Street London W1D 5AF   020 7439 0450
Locanda Locatelli   8 Seymour Street London W1H 7JZ   020 7935 9088
Lute Restaurant   Oude Molen 5, 1184VW Ouderkerk a/d Amstel Netherlands   +31(0)20 4722462
Mallory Court Hotel   Harbury Lane, Bishops Tachbrook, Leamington Spa Warwickshire CV33 9QB   01926 330 214
McClements   2 Whitton Road London TW1 1BJ   020 8744 9610
Mirabelle   56 Curzon Street London W1J 8PA   020 7499 4636

Momo   25 Heddon Street London 4BH   020 7434 4040

Moro   34-36 Exmouth Market London EC1R 4QE   020 7833 8336

Morston Hall   Morston, Holt Norfolk NR25 7AA   01263 741 041

Mosimann's   11b West Halkin Street London SW1X 8JL   020 7235 9625

Nahm   The Halkin 5 Halkin Street London SW1X 7DJ   020 7333 1234

Neal Street Restaurant   26 Neal Street London WC2H 9PS   020 7836 8368

Nick Nairn Cook School   Port of Menteith Stirling FK8 3JZ   01877 389 900

Nobu   Metropolitan Hotel 19 Old Park Lane London W1Y 4LB   020 7447 4747

Notting Grill   123A Clarendon Road London W11 4JG 020 7229 1500

Orrery   55-57 Marylebone High Street London W1U 5HS   020 7616 8000

Oxo Tower   Oxo Tower Wharf Barge House Street London SE1 9PH   020 7803 3888

Petersham Nursery   Off Petersham Road, Richmond Surrey TW10 7AW   020 8940 5230

Pool Court   at 42 44 The Calls Leeds LS2 7EW   0113 244 4242

Port-na-Craig   Portnacraig, Pitlochhry Perthshire PH16 5ND   01796 472 777

Providores   109 Marylebone High Street London W1U 4RX   020 7935 6175

Racine   239 Brompton Road London SW3 2EP   020 7584 4477

Rhodes Twenty Four Tower   42, 25 Old Broad Street London EC2N 1HQ   020 7877 7703

River Café   Thames Wharf, Rainville Road London   W6 9HA   020 7386 4200

River Cottage   Bridport Dorset www.rivercottage.net

Smiths of Smithfield   67-77 Charterhouse Street London EC1M 6HJ   020 7251 7950

St John   26 St John Street   London   EC1M 4AY   020 7251 0848

Tamarind   20 Queen Street London W1J 5PR   020 7629 3561

Tavola   155 Westbourne Grove London W11 2RS   020 7229 0571

The Castle   Castle Green, Taunton Somerset TA1 1NF   01823 272671

The Connaught   The Connaught Hotel Carlos Place London W1K 2AL 020 7592 1222

The Fat Duck   High Street, Bray Berkshire SL6 2AQ   01628 580 333

The Ivy   1 West Street, Covent Garden London WC2H 9NQ   020 7836 4751

The Merchant House   Lower Corve Street, Ludlow Shropshire SY8 1DU   01584 875 438

The Real Greek   14-15 Hoxton Market London N1 6HG   020 7739 8212

The Seafood Restaurant   Riverside, Padstow Cornwall PL28 8BY   01841 532700

The Three Chimneys   Colbost, Dunvegan Isle of Skye IV55 8ZT   01470 511 258

The Vineyard at Stockcross   Newbury Berkshire RG20 8JU   01635 528 770

Thyme   The Hospital 24 Endell Street London WC2H 9HQ   020 7170 9200

Tom Aikens   43 Elystan Street London   SW3 3NT   020 7584 2003

Tom's   127 Westbourne Park Road London W2 5QL   020 7727 6771

Valvona & Crolla Caffè Bar   19 Elm Row Edinburgh EH7 4AA   0131 556 6066

Villandry   170 Great Portland Street London W1W 5QB   020 7631 3131

Whatley Manor   Easton Grey, Malmesbury Wiltshire SN16 0RB   01666 822 888

Winteringham Fields   Winteringham Lincolnshire DN15 9PF   01724 733 096

Wolseley   160 Piccadilly London W1J 9EB   020 7499 6996

Yauatcha   15-17 Broadwick Street London W1F 0DL   020 7494 8888

Index

The Charities

"Up to 52,000 young people are estimated to have been 'found homeless' by local authorities in England in 2003." (source: research commissioned by Centrepoint and conducted by York University) This is about 1 in 60 of all 15-19 year-olds in England, or the total number of all 15-19 year olds living in a major city such as Leeds.

"In 2003, one in four (27%) of all Salvation Army clients had significant mental health problems – (that's approximately 1,000 people a year in hostels or a quarter of the population of our 50 residential centres). Among its own clients, The Salvation Army has also found that 61% of clients have an alcohol dependency and 54% have problems with Class A drugs."
(source: The Salvation Army)

Our aim in compiling Soup Kitchen is to raise funds for charities which care about and act on homelessness in the UK. Rather than reinforcing stereotypes of soup and homelessness, we hope that this book will translate a widespread contemporary interest in food and healthy living into funds for invaluable short-term and long-term homeless projects.

70% of all money raised from sales of Soup Kitchen and all related promotional activities will be donated to charities who work to support homeless people in London and around the UK.

Our main beneficiaries include:

The Salvation Army
Registered Charity No. 214779
www.salvationarmy.org.uk
T 0845 634 0101

Centrepoint
Registered Charity No. 292411
www.centrepoint.org.uk
T 0207 426 5300

These charities support the homeless on many different levels, from influencing public policy to the provision of direct services (housing, health, education, counselling, support and training). They are committed to finding ways to support individuals who, for a variety of reasons, have no home and often have nowhere else to turn.

In addition, we will be donating to a variety of other charities, both large and small, whose incredible work we support passionately. For further information on the work of all charities involved with Soup Kitchen and fundraising activities and progress, please see www.soupkitchen.org

McDermott, Will & Emery are overseeing all legalities for charity contributions.